133 SKIING LESSONS

by JEAN-CLAUDE KILLY

Edited by Frank Covino

DBI BOOKS, INC., NORTHFIELD, ILLINOIS
(Formerly Digest Books, Inc.)

- *Instruction by* **Jean-Claude Killy**

- *Edited by* **Frank Covino**

- *Illustrations by* **Anthony Ravielli**

- *Photos by* **John C. Russell**

- *Editorial Production by* **Wanda Sahagian**

- *Publisher:* **Sheldon L. Factor**

Published by DBI Books, Inc., a subsidiary of Technical Publishing Co., 540 Frontage Rd., Northfield, Illinois 60093.

ISBN 0-695-80628-9   Library of Congress Catalog Card #75-18011

About Jean-Claude Killy

In 1946, when Robert Killy closed his bicycle business and moved his young family to the Haute Savoie Mountain village of Val d'Isere, little did he know that his change in lifestyle would also change the course of skiing history. From the tiny acorn grows the mighty oak, and so it would be with the career of his then three-year-old son, Jean-Claude.

Skiing in Val d'Isere is like stickball in Brooklyn and basketball in Indiana—everyone does it. In fact, when the heavy snows hit Val d'Isere, skiing is often the most convenient mode of transportation, and it was therefore not unusual that Jean-Claude began his skiing career not long after taking his first steps. He started skiing at three and by the time he received his first pair of skis, was so involved with the sport that his parents nicknamed him *Toutoune*, a "crazy dog," totally obsessed by sking.

In most places, parents are happy to see their children become involved in sports since it "keeps them off the streets." In Killy's early years, however, his love for skiing seemed to bring him nothing but trouble, since he soon became adept at playing hooky so that he could have more time on the slopes. He vividly recalls one Thursday (church day in Val d'Isere) when, instead of being in the chapel with his peers, he was sailing freely down the slopes—that is until the village priest ("unfortunately a faster skier than me in those days") swept down on him and escorted him (quite painfully) by his ear to rejoin his compatriots.

Although, at a very young age, Jean-Claude began to show the signs of a future champion (he scored his first alpine triple victory at the age of ten), his father became concerned that too much skiing was retarding his social and intellectual development and that the constant physical exertion was robbing him of the energy which he needed to grow. Killy was, in fact, a "late bloomer" and, with the exception of his skiing, a shy and retiring boy who was so small for his age that his friends, although they respected his skiing ability, dubbed him *Le Petit Killy*.

It was with these concerns that Robert Killy made the painful decision to send his son to a boarding school away from the mountains. Jean-Claude remembers his eleventh and twelfth years as the worst period of his life, a time during which he was so depressed that he became ill and contracted a severe pulmonary infection, diagnosed as tuberculosis, which kept him in the hospital for four months, after which his doctors ordered that he do no skiing for the period of one year. To remove the temptation, Jean-Claude was sent even further from the mountains, to a second school in Voiron. Separated from the lifestyle which represented freedom and happiness, he was miserable and vowed to make up for lost time when he got out.

At age thirteen, Jean-Claude transferred to a school closer to the mountains and, in his spare time, resumed his skiing with such intensity that nobody around Val d'Isere could keep up with him and he was allowed to train with the French B Team. Early that year, Jean-Claude was invited to participate in the Ilio Colli Cup at Cortina d'Ampezzo,

Italy. Despite a denial of permission from parents and school, Jean-Claude headed for Italy with the team and suffered the ignominious rewards of a fractured leg and dismissal from school. What appeared to be a tragedy, turned to fortune. During the few months of recuperation, Jean-Claude had grown six inches! Whether this was vindication of Robert Killy's "hyperactivity" theory or just a chance coincidence between the injury and a late maturity is irrelevant: Jean-Claude was no longer the "Petit Killy" and now had the size and strength to be a contender in international competition.

In 1960, Jean-Claude swept the French Junior Nations at La Clusaz and, as the result of this and other surprising finishes, was given the unprecedented opportunity to train with the French A Team at the age of sixteen. As a racer, Killy was something else. He was fast, but the skiing establishment shook its collective head at what they called his "brink of disaster" technique. He sat back, skied on his uphill ski, hunched over—perfectly acceptable technique now, but then considered cardinal sins in skiing. At that time, heavy emphasis was put on form. Jean-Claude defied tradition and aimed directly at the heart of the matter: To him the thrill in skiing was speed and speed wins races—so ski fast. He learned primarily through the "do it yourself" method, taking the very best from others and not being afraid to innovate. The experts of that period sighed, "he'd be fantastic," and seemed to be right at the time since Jean-Claude, although fast, was far from consistent. It never dawned on anyone that he was exploring new frontiers in skiing speed. It was during the next year, in January of 1961, that Jean-Claude won his first international victory, the slalom at the Grand Prix de Morzine. In December of that year, he won his first major international event, the Criterium de la Premiere Neige at Val d'Isere—from 39th place by more than a second!

It was shortly following this "coming of age," that Jean-Claude suffered a series of setbacks: A broken leg in the downhill at, ironically, the Ilio Colli at Cortina and a bout with dysentery, which he contracted during his military service in Algeria the following summer—an ailment initially diagnosed as jaundice which persisted through the 1963-64 season. Despite these handicaps, Jean-Claude made the French Olympic Team and competed in the 1964 Olympics at Innsbruck, picking up a fifth in the giant slalom after falls in the downhill and slalom. It was his poor physical condition, and not unusual technique, which was holding Killy back, and the dismal showing in those Olympics turned out to be his last major disappointment in ski racing.

Following the Olympics and prior to the commencement of the 1964-65 season, a significant development occurred which virtually assured Jean-Claude's future chances of success. His old friend and French team associate, Michel Arpin, was appointed technical advisor to the Dynamic Ski Company and, from that time on, particularly after a serious auto accident ended his competitive skiing career, Arpin worked closely with Killy as trainer, equipment manager, mentor and coach, lifting Jean-Claude's spirits when needed, and working to provide him with the very best equipment in the very best condition, thereby freeing his mind to concentrate totally on winning races.

During the next two years, Jean-Claude was the terror of the slalom and giant slalom trails—and of the staid management of posh ski resorts as well! He became the French team's leading prankster and clown—always striking when least expected. He casually lost his pants in mid-air during a jumping exhibition, wore a sweatshirt marked "Courtesy of State Prison" in the dining room, drove a VW into the lobby of a hotel where the team was staying, and developed a deadly aim with seltzer bottles and water pistols. It was all very silly, but an ideal way to keep the growing pressure from press, fans, and rivals, from becoming overwhelming before the last pieces were in place. Killy had one unfinished task before he could lay claim to the title of the world's best skier—he had to become a master of skiing's premier event—the downhill. This breakthrough came in the summer of 1966 at the World Championships in Portillo, Chile. The idea of racing in a major competition when the slopes and trails of the Northern Hemisphere are green and bare of snow held little attraction for most top racers. Figuring that they would let down, Killy stepped up his training. He won the downhill decisively and, despite a slight case of "Montezuma's Revenge," did well enough in the other events to win the combined title.

Many, particularly the Austrians, denounced this victory as a fluke, but during the following season, Jean-Claude really hit stride and showed them how wrong they were. 1966-67 was the best season of Jean-Claude's career. It was the first year of the World Cup, the competition determining the best racer of the year on the basis of points awarded in key races throughout the season. Of the 17 races scheduled that year, Killy entered 16, winning all five downhills, four of five giant slaloms and three of six slaloms. Since only the three best results in each event counted towards the World Cup, he ended up with a perfect 225, a feat that has never been repeated. Along with other victories and high placings that year, it was probably the most brilliant season ever enjoyed by a ski racer.

After that season, the only ski worlds left to conquer were the Olympics—an Olympic gold medal is skiing's most prestigious trophy, three being the ultimate skiing achievement, a "grand slam." Once again, Killy did the unexpected: He ceased to be the happy-go-lucky fellow. For once in his life, he became deadly serious. He and Arpin prepared meticulously for the forthcoming season, testing and developing equipment to anticipate all possible contingencies, carefully alternating periods of intense training with relaxation and steadily sharpening Killy's racing skills so that he would be at his peak for the games. Since, during the 1960s, skiing had become a sport of specialization and the three event skier a vanishing breed, Jean-Claude's total sweep of the 1968 Olympic games at Grenoble, 25,000 cheering countrymen and Charles De Gaulle notwithstanding, ranks as one of the greatest athletic achievements of all time.

At the end of the 1968-69 season, and following his second consecutive World Cup victory, Jean-Claude, having conquered virtually every attainable milestone in amateur skiing, made the decision to turn professional and capitalize upon his fame and glory. The only trouble with being a professional skier in 1969 was that there was only a very limited forum in which to compete, so Killy did the next best thing: He capitalized on his hard-earned fame and endorsed a select assortment of ski equipment and clothing; made personal and television appearances; promoted automobiles and ski tours and wrote articles for skiing magazines and other publications.

The next five years saw Killy as a star, both in and out of his element. He was seen in the jetstreams of the world, sharing the company of famous men and beautiful women, including his present wife, Daniele Gaubert. He dabbled in motor racing and became the star of two television shows: "The Killy Challenge," an exciting format in which challengers received a handicap and a chance at $10,000 if they could beat Jean-Claude (nobody collected) and the "Killy Style," a series in which Jean-Claude travelled around the world, skiing exotic places such as the Nguarhoe Volcano and Tasman Glacier of New Zealand and the "Four Walls" of Chamonix. He also used this period to launch a movie career via his starring role in the Warner Bros. movie, "Snow Job."

In the fall of 1972, Killy, much concerned that he was rapidly fading into the obscurity of the record books and Skiing Hall of Fame, and feeling confident that he could equal or surpass his past skiing achievements, made the courageous decision to return to serious international skiing competition by joining the International Ski Racers Association tour, skiing's rapidly growing counterpart to the PGA in golf. Killy bet on himself—and won. Over the course of one ski season, racers and skiing public alike watched with amazement as rusty Killy, who barely qualified in his first two professional races, rapidly transformed himself into *Le Champion* of old. He went on to win more professional giant slaloms than any of his competitors, more than his share of slaloms and ultimately captured the 1972-73 World Professional Championship, defeating Austrian star, Harald Stuefer and America's two-time world professional champion, Spider Sabich.

Whatever his chosen field of endeavor, Jean-Claude Killy is out to win. He is as keen at a business conference as he is on the slopes. He is a self-made millionaire, rapidly becoming a one-man conglomerate. In addition to having his own line of skis, ski apparel and ski poles, he serves as a consultant to several companies both in and out of the ski industry, lending his name, knowledge and promotional expertise to those who value him increasingly for what he *is* and what he *can do* rather than for what he was and did.

Despite his many accomplishments, Jean-Claude still prefers the company of his old friends and has not forgotten the people who gave him his start, particularly the people of Val d'Isere, where he spends a good deal of his time and owns a ski shop which is operated by his father and younger brother.

Although his self-image is no longer that of a ski racer, "self-fulfillment" remains the watchword of Jean-Claude Killy and no matter which path he shall choose to pursue, you can be assured that the high-energy perfectionist will bring to it the same excellence which has characterized his career as a skier.

Michael W. Halstead

TABLE OF CONTENTS

SECTION 3—THE ADVANCED SKIER

SECTION 4—QUESTIONS AND ANSWERS

Introduction

Hello my friends! If you are a veteran skier, it's good to see you again. If you are a beginner, welcome to skiing and congratulations. You may not be aware of it as yet, but you are not only learning a sport, but adopting a unique, exhilarating and, believe me, all-encompassing life-style which (if you are like me and most skiers) will add a new dimension to your life. How many people do you know who have skied *once* and then quit? Like eating that American potato chip, I am willing to bet that once will not be enough—it never is. That is, unless you are allergic to feeling good and having fun. Since I have grown up on skis and owe virtually everything I have to skiing, you may consider me less than objective, but a vast majority of the skiers who I have encountered (particularly in North America) have taken up the sport relatively late in life and enjoy it all the more. On the other hand, the fact that I have skied since age three and still enjoy it immensely (and intend to as long as I am able to strap on a pair of skis) is a testimony to skiing's endearing and enduring nature. On the off-chance that you have not yet decided whether or not you want to become a skier, just let me say this: With recent developments in ski instruction, ski area maintenance and technological developments in skiing equipment, skiing is no longer a daredevil enterprise for the young and lion-hearted. The visions of the man with his leg in a cast and the St. Bernard with the cask of brandy around its neck are now outdated cliches and should be replaced by a picture of people of all ages, sizes, shapes and temperaments enjoying an activity with lifetime application, community spirit, a direct benefit to their health and well-being and a communication with nature. To me, skiing is all this and more. It is the unique ambiance of the ski resort, the intimate communication between the skier, his equipment and the snow, the excitement of travel to and from the ski area and the sensations of mobility, gravity and speed one experiences while sliding down the hill. It is the indescribable sensation of liberation and freedom one gets from escaping to a new and unique environment where traditional social labels fall by the wayside and people form a common bond through shared activity. It is health, suntan, a hot buttered rum by the fireside on a cold winter's night. In short, it is the best way to turn those long, dreary winter months into your favorite time of the year.

As you know, since the end of the 1968 ski season, I have earned my livelihood as a professional skier. During this period, I have been very grateful for having the opportunity to transmit my knowledge and philosophy of skiing to the public through my widely syndicated newspaper series, "Skiing With Jean-Claude Killy." Over the course of the more than six years in which this series has been published, I have endeavored to set forth, as clearly and concisely as possible, a series of instructional tips, ranging from the most fundamental maneuvers such as walking on skis, to the most complex, i.e., alpine racing. The series deals not only with the all important basic fundamentals of skiing technique, but addresses itself to those special situations one encounters in the sport, e.g., skiing on powder and ice, and how they should be dealt with by skiers at all levels of proficiency.

Since preparation is half the battle in achieving safety and enjoyment in skiing, I have provided you with the basic information you will need regarding physical conditioning and equipment selection and preparation to help assure your chances of success in mastering the basics of the sport and enjoying it to the maximum extent possible.

Furthermore, it is my feeling that a knowledgeable skier is a better and happier one and it is with this objective in mind that I have attempted to provide bits of education regarding the evolution of the sport and the many forms which it now takes.

Although I certainly hope that the series has been helpful to those who have read it faithfully since its first publication in 1968, it has occurred to me that, since I have now touched virtually upon all aspects of the sport, the time is right to put these various writings into logical order and make them available to you in one work. Hence: 133 Ski Lessons by Jean-Claude Killy.

Let's face it: Even though I have tried to make these various articles as readable and interesting as possible, a ski instructional series is, by its nature, a far cry from your average adventure story. If it's exciting reading you are after, put me back on the shelf; if it's exciting *skiing*, read on *mon ami*, read on! By applying the contents of this book to your skiing, you will find that the obstacles to your progress will fall by the wayside with amazing speed.

One final point: Don't be afraid to learn if you are a beginner and don't let your ego block your path to excellence if you are an experienced skier. In reviewing my long career, I have come to the conclusion that my greatest moments in skiing took place when I conquered new frontiers. Whether your new frontier is mastering the snow plow turn at your local ski area or charging down the Matterhorn is irrelevant: It is the self-realization and the feeling of setting new goals and conquering them, not the relative magnitude of those goals, which is important and satisfying. A good mountain climber exults not only in the brief period when he has conquered the mountain, but along every step of the way. Similarly, in skiing, every small increment of improvement is yet another victory, and if you maintain this philosophy, you will enjoy all phases of your skiing experience. Good luck and happy skiing.

Jean-Claude Killy

1-Beginner & Novice

SOME WORDS FOR FIRST TIME SKIERS

I want to talk to you people who have never skied but want to get started. I certainly offer encouragement because skiing has been a deeply satisfying part of my life.

And it's fun. You can see in this picture that I'm full of *joie de vivre*. I'm doing what is called the Jet Christie and when you know how, it's easy. But you don't need to be an expert for skiing to be fun. In fact, it can be rewarding from the very first day. You'll find you enjoy learning, and as you learn more you can then take on gradually bigger challenges. That's where the excitement comes in!

You might begin by going to a specialty ski shop to look around at the equipment and clothes and ask a few questions. You'll probably find that most people at the shop will agree with me and say that your boots are the most important part of your equipment. They must fit properly, give you support and be comfortable. So, look at the boots, safety bindings and other equipment.

For your first time on skis, pick an area with a ski school. Most of these areas have experienced instructors, but check on this. I certainly recommend that you take a lesson as soon as you get to the ski area.

I stress ski school because you will have more fun and satisfaction by progressing faster. And you will be much safer. The risk of injury is slight, but it is reduced even more by beginning at a school. Perhaps your friends who already ski will want to teach you. But remember, in the hands of a ski instructor you will be exposed to someone who has personally helped hundreds of first-day skiers like yourself get off to a good start.

TUNE UP BEFORE YOU CUT LOOSE ON THE SLOPES

I have had few accidents during my very active racing career. I attribute this to some simple precautionary habits. One of these has been to thoroughly warm up before cutting loose on the slopes.

A very important part of my warm-up routine consists of stretching exercises for all the big muscles of the body—the calves, the thighs, the hamstrings, the large muscles of the back and shoulders. Why? If your body is called upon to perform some extraordinary task, as it always is when you lose balance and strive to recover or when you take a tumble, the sudden wrench can easily tear muscles which haven't been warmed up and pre-stretched, so to speak. I certainly recommend that you spend at least half a minute or more, particularly after every cold trip up the mountain, to stretch and stimulate the flow of blood through the large muscles.

A few of my favorite "stretchers" are illustrated here. Let me comment briefly about them. In "A" I put my hands on my skis, close to the toes, or else grasp the ankles, striving to straighten my legs. This stretches the back of the legs, the back, and the neck. In "B," I squat, then force my seat to my heels in a series of quick up-and-down movements to stretch the muscles of the legs. While in the same position, I will often try to force my knees toward the skis to stretch the muscles of the lower leg. In "C," I twist while standing in place to stretch the muscles of the trunk. I'm sure you know many similar stretching exercises, so use them.

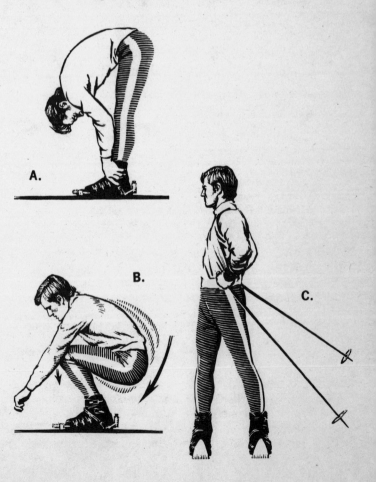

CHOOSE THE RIGHT CLOTHES
FOR SKIING

Ski clothing should keep you warm but not over-warm. It must allow you to move freely in this active sport yet be made durably. After these conditions are met, you can then pick from the wide variety of colors and styles that make skiers a colorful lot.

Dress in layers . . . several light layers will keep you warmer than one or two heavy ones. If you find that you are too warm, you can shed one of the thin layers, or if you are too cold, you can add another underneath.

Let's get specific. On your feet you will want thin cotton or wool socks and thick wool ones on top. On your legs, long underwear under your ski pants. The long underwear not only keeps you warm, it adds a little padding to make falling softer. You'll fall . . . all skiers do, even me. On your top you'll want a turtleneck shirt with an undershirt beneath. Some skiers like the fishnet type of undershirt while others prefer a conventional cotton or cotton/wool.

Next you'll want a light or medium weight wool sweater, then a parka. Make sure that the parka is made specially for skiing. There are a lot of "ski look" parkas on the market which don't have the durability and freedom of movement features that a real ski parka should have. A supplement to your parka which is handy to have, but not essential, is a nylon windshirt. If the weather is nice and warm, you can wear the windshirt over (or under) your sweater and go without your parka. If it's very cold you can wear the windshirt under your parka as an added layer.

Body heat is lost quickly through a bare head so a hat is important in keeping not only your head and ears, but all of you warm. Knit hats are practical and come in a wide variety of styles and colors. Fur, fake fur and helmet type hats are also popular. Any hat that you get should be able to come down over the ears.

On your hands you'll need special ski mittens or gloves. They are made of special leather and are snug around the wrist to keep snow out. Mittens are warmer than gloves, so if your hands get cold easily, you might prefer them. Most skiers prefer gloves because of their flexibility. Ski gloves are usually lined with foam or other special materials.

So now, I've suited you up for skiing from top to toe. But let me emphasize the importance of being dressed right for the temperature. If you are too warm and sweat too much, your clothes will get damp and lose their insulating properties. As soon as you stop moving you can get thoroughly chilled because of these damp clothes. If you aren't dressed warmly enough you are also asking for trouble. Cold muscles don't react well and you are more apt to fall. And if you do take a bad fall your stiffer joints and muscles are more prone to strains and sprains. So, keep warm, *mes amis.*

THIS IS YOUR ALPINE EQUIPMENT

Alpine skiing is the kind where you ride uphill in mechanical comfort and then enjoy the thrill of coming down under gravity-power alone. Turning is everything in Alpine skiing. You control your speed, avoid obstacles, and stop by turning.

As a result, all of your running gear—skis, bindings, boots—are designed for that purpose. Your skis have to be very strong—they must endure sheer forces of more than one ton. Your bindings must hold you forcefully, yet release when the loads get to dangerous levels. And your boots must support your foot and ankle very firmly, for they must withstand forces several times your weight.

During recent years, manufacturers have made remarkable progress in the specialized designs for Alpine skiing. That is a large part of the reason why there have been so many refinements in today's ski techniques. Here is some general information for you about equipment.

BOOTS FOR ALPINE COMPETITORS: They reach high up the calf and pitch your lower leg forward nearly 25 degrees. They do not permit much movement of the lower legs; so the skier can instantly apply pressure to any portion of the skis. They tire the legs, and are for experts only.

BOOTS FOR RECREATIONAL SKIERS: These must fit perfectly. They should allow some back and forward hinging action at the ankle, and they should be neither too high nor slanted forward too much, so that the legs will not have to endure strain just to stand up.

SKIS FOR ALPINE COMPETITORS: For the downhill, they must be at least one foot longer than head-height, relatively wide all along their length, and generally stiffer bending, to handle high speeds. For giant slalom, they should be about five inches shorter and less stiff. For slalom, they must be light, easier bending and three inches shorter than giant slalom skis.

SKIS FOR RECREATION SKIERS: Expert recreation skiers may use either slalom or giant slalom skis, but one size (about two inches) shorter than for racing. The average recreation skier should use a so-called "Combi" ski—a design half-way between the slalom and giant slalom models. And since these skiers seldom ski faster than 25 mph, there is no need for them to use a ski any longer than they are tall.

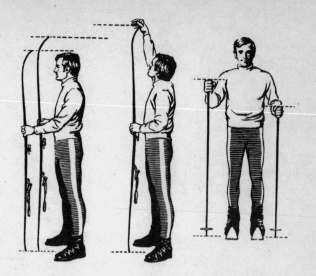

EQUIPMENT—THE LONG AND THE SHORT OF IT

I am often asked about ski equipment and, in particular, about the proper length of poles and skis. Well, just about every expert has his opinion on the matter, and I'm no exception. But I will try to give you enough guidance here so you can make your own decision.

SKIS—you can see, from the illustrations, what is meant by a long ski. The shortest ski shown is just that—short. The intermediate length shown is about right for most people.

If you are a beginner or are not particularly athletic, I suggest a length which reaches to within an inch or two above the top of your head. This length provides all the stability you'll need, since you won't be skiing fast; at the same time, turns are easier than with longer skis. Preferably, skis any shorter than your height should only be used with the supervision of your instructor or by persons who have no opportunity to get into enough shape to enjoy the sport to its utmost.

If you are an intermediate skier, then choose a ski 3, 6, 9, or even 12 inches taller than your height. Choose the shorter options if you are either short, lightweight, not expertly coordinated, or not in especially great shape. Choose the longer options if you are the opposite of those characteristics.

If you are an expert, you will use long skis, 12, 15, even 18 inches higher than your height.

POLES—Some great racers I know like to use long poles, that is, ones that reach to the armpit or higher. But give me the short pole—one that reaches to just above my waist, with the tip not stuck into the snow when I am standing on my skis. I seem to need the quick maneuverability I get from this length. What's right for you? Not likely anything proportionately more than an inch or two shorter than mine, and perhaps something proportionately a couple of inches longer. If you are unsure, why not buy a pair of poles that are on the long side and have them cut down an inch at a time by your ski shop until you find the length you like? I know your skiing will improve once you find your own ideal length for skis and poles. *Bonne chance.*

CHOOSING THE SKIS THAT ARE RIGHT FOR YOU

For your first few times on the snow, almost any ski will do—ideally, not more than three to six inches taller than you are. In fact, if you start with a ski that barely reaches to your chin, you'll find learning quite easy. There are even some ski schools that start adults off on skis as short as four feet. Because there is so much to learn about ski equipment, I recommend that you rent skis and boots for your first few sessions. Then, while you are skiing, ask your ski instructor and friends about the kind of skis which would be exactly right for you.

There are many kinds of skis, and each of them is best suited for a certain kind of skier. There are skis made of wood, skis made of wood and aluminum and skis made of glass and metal. Prices range from a low of $20 to a high of $250. For your first season of skiing you may be able to get by with an inexpensive model—under $60. But if you intend to budget more than that for your first pair of skis, by all means find out from people who know more about what you should buy. In the end, of course, you will have to decide for yourself; but the more information you've gathered, the easier that will be.

For most skiers, a very important matter in the choice of skis is the bending flex of a ski. Here, you see me stressing a ski to test its flex. In the large illustration, my hand—the one grasping the ski's waist—is pushing at right angles to the ski. In the small illustration, I am stressing the shovel area of the ski to feel how stiff it is. Each type of ski has its own characteristic feel, and most good skiers have taught themselves to feel out the ski that is just right for them. Unless you are very heavy or very strong and athletic, do *not* choose a ski which is too stiff. To do so is to court unpleasant skiing. Another way to get a feeling for the stiffness or flexibility of a pair of skis is to stand them up bottom to bottom. If you cannot take all of the arch (camber) out of them by squeezing with one hand and causing the bottoms to touch along their entire running surface length, then chances are the ski is too stiff for you.

Choosing skis just right for you will become easier once you learn what flex you like and are able to feel it out for yourself, in the way I have demonstrated here.

BOOT UP RIGHT

Ever notice what a ski racer does just moments after crossing the finish line? Sure, he may collapse on the snow to give himself a few moments of very heavy gasping for breath to reinstate an oxygen balance. But almost invariably, he reaches down and unclips the buckles of his boots because he had clasped them shut painfully tight just before the start of the race. A ski racer demands the instant response of his skis, and the only way to get that is through an almost direct linkage from bone and muscle through his ski boots to the edges of his skis.

Such a painful connection is not necessary, of course, when skiing for fun, but it *is* necessary to have a very close fitting boot if you expect to have any kind of quick response from your skis. For that reason, in this lesson, I'm reviewing some of the important steps which are needed to make your boots fit more snugly.

First, be sure your socks are pulled up snugly around your toes and heel. Then, once the foot has been inserted in the boot, tug upwards on the inner boot to remove any creases caused when your foot was inserted. Now, if possible, fasten the buckle that crosses high on the instep—usually the 4th one from the bottom. Then flex your ankle by pushing the knee forward. This should force your heel to seat itself properly in its boot pocket. Finally buckle up from the bottom-most fastener and retighten the fourth one, if necessary. Should this procedure fail to seat your heel properly, then try this:

With all buckles unfastened, kick back only the heel of the boot, forcing your heel to seat itself. Then, while keeping the boot toe off the ground, buckle up from the bottom. With a little practice you will learn to buckle your feet in firmly—and comfortably, applying full pressure only if you're going out to win on the race course.

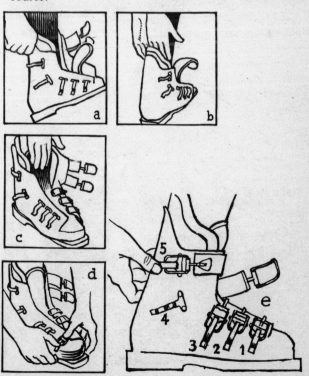

WHERE TO MOUNT YOUR BINDINGS

I don't believe that many recreational skiers know much about where, exactly, to mount bindings on a new pair of skis. It makes a difference, believe me, because your skis won't behave properly if the bindings are too far forward or too far back.

If you are going to mount bindings on your skis yourself, here's what you should know. First, I will mention that the bindings go on top of the skis. But aside from that, the correct placement of the binding should result in having the center of the ball of your foot over the center of the running surface of the ski. You can see the location of this point in the illustration.

A good, yet simple, method for finding the proper placement point on your skis is this:

(a) As shown in the illustration, measure the straight-line distance from the tip back to the tail of the ski.

(b) Then divide this distance by two and you have the point which the toe of your ski boot should touch. If the toe of your foot rests far back from the toe of the boot, then you'll have to mount the bindings slightly ahead to compensate.

The formula I have given to you is, by and large, what most specialty ski shops use, and I can recommend it to you. But I also know that placing the bindings is far from an exact science. Often I have had to move the bindings a little forward or a little back to get them placed exactly right for me and a particular ski. Racers alter the formula to fit their special needs. For slalom the binding would be placed about a half-inch in front of the formula midpoint and for downhill racing, back from the midpoint about half an inch.

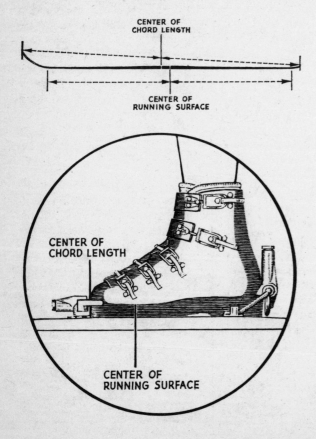

CENTER OF
CHORD LENGTH

CENTER OF
RUNNING SURFACE

CENTER OF
CHORD LENGTH

CENTER OF
RUNNING SURFACE

GET A PROPER GRIP ON YOUR POLES

Very early in my career, I lost a race because I was careless about how I gripped my poles. I had allowed my leather straps to stretch so much that when the tip of my pole held to the snow more than I expected it to, the pole was wrenched free of my hand. Ever since then, you can believe that I make sure that the straps fit tightly—are short enough to fit as snugly to my hand as my hand fits my glove.

Many ski instructors have told me how important it is for novice skiers to hold their poles right. When they don't, the fingers have to squeeze the grip and this tenses up the arm and makes all movements stiff. I know that if an advanced skier hasn't a good grip on his poles, he won't be able to rely on their support during *le moment critique*—that critical moment that occurs every time you make a fast, sharp turn. Here's how you should grip your poles:

1. If the strap is leather, give the smooth side a half twist inwards so that the loop formed will rest smooth and flat around your glove. Some of the poles which now come with plastic straps have them pre-twisted to conform to your grip. Always slip your hand, including the thumb, through the loop made by the strap by passing it up from underneath.

2. Then pull back on the strap so it rests against the back of your hand.

3. Grasp the pole with your thumb on one side, fingers on the other. Both parts of the strap should now rest between your hand and the pole.

4. Now press down on the strap to take up any slack. The top of your hand **with the glove on** should now rest no more than one-half-inch from the top of the ski pole. If more of the pole protrudes above the top of your hand, then the strap should be shortened.

YOUR FIRST STEPS ON SKIS

For those of you who will be skiing for the first time, I would like to teach you how to take your first steps. Even if you have skied before you might spot something to improve upon in the way you glide on your skis.

Actually, I can tell a great deal about a skier's ability just by watching him walk along a flat area of snow. If he is stiff like a tin soldier and if he is making hard work out of what should be an easy gliding walk, then I know that he doesn't feel at home on his skis. Remember, walking on level snow with your skis should be easier and faster than walking on snow with your skis off. If it's not, you are doing something wrong.

For your premiere in the snow, pick a place to practice which is flat, with no slope. First try walking without planting your poles in the snow so you can concentrate on what you are doing with your legs and skis. (Just let the poles trail along behind.) Your feet should be comfortably apart . . . 6 to 8 inches should be right. The skis should be parallel. Now slide one ski forward in your first step and follow with the other in a natural walking rhythm. Don't pick the ski up to move it forward, slide it forward with a thrusting movement.

As you see in the illustration, I bend the knee of my forward leg as I walk; I'm not stiff legged. Also, notice where I am looking. My head is up and I'm looking in front of me, not down at my feet and skis. As you walk, focus your eyes on some object in front of you (for myself, a pretty girl might serve the purpose) and you won't get in the habit of looking down. Also notice that I'm taking a nice long stride which helps me slide forward and gets me where I'm going faster and easier. Most beginners take short little steps and don't really slide forward with the front foot as I am doing. Actually, if the illustration was a motion picture, you would see that I slide on my front or thrusting foot and push with my back foot. Then, when the front foot loses momentum it stops on the snow and becomes the pushing foot as I slide forward on my other foot. Also notice that I have my upper body inclined slightly forward. This helps keep my forward momentum going.

After you feel that you are doing pretty well walking without the aid of your poles, start using them. They will help you push yourself forward and also help your balance. To do this place the pole opposite the lead foot into the snow behind the heel of the lead foot, as you see me doing in the illustration. Also notice that I have the pole on an angle, slanting backwards. The placement and the angle allow me to push with my arm, shoulder and back. If the pole were planted further forward and not angled, I'd have to pull on it and that's much harder work. As you push off with this pole your back leg will be coming up to take over the lead position and you'll then plant the other pole in the same manner. The movement is really a natural one, it's the same arm and leg alternation that you use on "dry land."

If you practice what I have told you in this lesson, you'll find that walking on skis is not only easy, it's fun.

HOW TO GET UP AFTER A FALL

The way you fall and the way I fall are entirely different. As a racer and even as a pleasure skier, the last thing I want to do is go for a tumble in the snow. After all, as they say, if you don't fall, you don't get hurt. If you are in shape, getting up from a fall is no big deal. But if you're not, it's not so easy. If you are in really poor condition, it's almost impossible, sometimes. To get an idea of how difficult it might be, sprawl on the floor and then try to get to your feet. Complicate the situation by trying to get up from the floor with poles in hand, skis on your feet.

At first, it's always difficult to get up on snow unless you realize that your skis will tend to run away from you even on the flat. But, practice and know-how conquers all. And if you have trouble, a friendly ski instructor will surely help you to your feet. Sooner or later, though, you'll have to learn to do it yourself. Here's the easiest way I know.

First, get your skis below you. Then place them across the slope so they are perpendicular to the line going from the top of the slope to the bottom . . . the fall line. With your skis across the slope they won't take off down the hill, forward or backward, when you get back up on them.

Now get your feet underneath your hips so that your weight will be directly over your feet as you get up. Next place your ski poles side by side in the snow by your uphill hip. Hold them together with your uphill hand down by the baskets and with the other hand, holding the ends of the grips.

Now, as you push up with the aid of your poles, roll your weight back over your skis and move your lower hand up the poles as you get more upright. Then stand up and catch your breath.

Getting up is not easy at first, but with practice, your strength and coordination will improve and it will be less difficult.

HOW TO FALL SAFELY

Every skier falls, even I do. The important thing is to fall properly so you avoid injury. Let me show you how.

Start by sitting back, as if you were going to sit down, as you see me doing in the first drawing of the sequence above. But don't sit all the way down on your skis or you'll be taken for a toboggan ride. Keep your hands up and your poles pointing rearward. If a pole is pointing in front of you, the tip may catch in the snow and your hand and the pole may be forced back and bump you in the head.

At the last split second as you are sitting down, move your *derriere* off to the side and sit down on the snow. (See the second and third illustrations.) Because most of your weight will now be on your seat, you can keep your skis parallel and their tips free from the snow to avoid their catching and digging in. The same goes for your knees . . . keep them up and free of the snow or one might dig in the snow and turn your graceful little fall into an "egg beater," a dangerous rolling tumble.

If you are heading across a hill when you do your fall, sit down to the uphill side of your skis and you won't have to fall as far. I urge you to practice falling safely. It does wonders for your confidence. And every skier needs plenty of that.

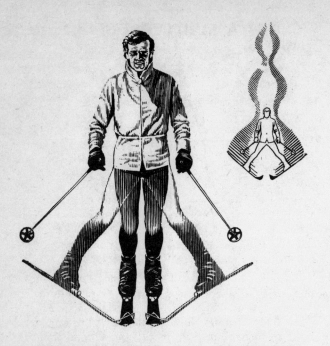

SNOWPLOWING, THE ACTION TO TAKE WHEN YOU WANT TO BRAKE

I don't make a habit of snowplowing. It slows you down and that's the last thing any racer wants to have happen. The snowplow is a braking maneuver. In this lesson, you see me standing directly over my skis as if I were sliding straight down the fall line. The extra legs superimposed on the figure show the tails of my skis pushed out into the classic snowplow V-position with the tips no more than a few inches apart and the skis resting on their inside edges. Note that my body is properly centered over both skis, to keep my weight distributed equally on each ski.

To learn to snowplow, first practice on the flat where there is no possibility of sliding forward or backward. Step your skis—one at a time—into the proper position. Then practice hopping both skis simultaneously into a snowplow position, than back into schussing position. Many ski instructors would prefer that you don't learn to snowplow until you already know how to traverse and sideslip, but this isn't always practical. At some ski areas, you have to know how to stop very early in the game. However, to be forewarned is to be fore-armed—so that I must tell you that practicing the snowplow for too long can cause you to develop a habit which may take years to get rid of. How long is too long? It might be as little as half an hour, or as much as a day or two. It's such an individual matter that only a very knowledgeable ski instructor can properly advise you. In any case, the moment to stop is when your first reaction to the slightest concern for your welfare is to snowplow.

You do gain a number of benefits by learning to snowplow. You learn independent leg action. You develop muscles to control your skis. You learn about edge control. And, you do learn how to come to a stop when skiing straight down a hill. The small diagram shows a valuable snowplow exercise. Ski straight down a gentle slope alternately pushing your heels apart and letting them come together again.

HOW TO CLIMB

How to climb up a hill on skis is something you have to know. Lifts can get you up to the top but sometimes you have to climb up to the lift. Also, climbing is a good practical exercise for learning how to feel at home on your skis and for developing your legs and ankles which are vital for the turning maneuvers. You also learn edge control.

There are several ways to climb with skis. The sidestep is one. It's like stepping sideways up a stair. Facing crossways to the hill, and with your feet together and skis parallel, you lift the uphill ski and move it sideways up the slope. Then you stand on this ski and move the bottom ski up next to it. Repeat this and you'll find yourself moving right up the hill. If the snow is hard or icy you'll have to slam your feet down hard as you move them sideways. This makes the steel edges bite into the snow so your skis won't slip out from under you as you take your next step. Also you'll edge your skis into the hill which is like walking on the sides of your feet. The downhill pole is the most important. Plant it next to your downhill foot with your hand next to your hip so you can push off from it as you climb. Keep the uphill pole out of the way of your ski as you move it sideways up the hill.

Then there's the half sidestep. Walk forward as you sidestep with your uphill foot. You will then be going up the hill diagonally. This is easier than going straight up . . . it's half walking forward and half climbing.

The herringbone, so called because of the track it makes in the snow (see illustration) is strenuous but it gets you directly and quickly up the hill. You face straight up the hill with your skis in a "V" position. First you lift one foot up then the other, walking on the inside edge of each ski. Notice how I hold my poles. I have the end of the poles in the bottom of each palm so the poles and my arm form a straight line and my hands are behind my hips so I am always able to push off from them. Then as I move one foot up I poke my pole in behind the moving foot so I can push myself up.

Climbing up the hill is a good way to "get the kinks out" before the first run of the day or after a cold chair-lift ride. It speeds the circulation and loosens up your muscles. So before you start your run down, go up the hill with a few quick climbing steps.

A HANDY POLE GRIP

In the small illustration, I am stepping around into position to head straight down the hill. You'll note that my hands appear to grip my ski poles in an unusual position. The illustration in the circle shows this grip, as viewed from behind. I've merely moved my hand upward, to receive the upper end of the plastic grip right into the little pocket in the palm of my hand. This not only effectively lengthens the reach of the arms and poles, it allows you to put almost the entire weight of your upper body onto the poles without tiring your arms. You can also use this grip when climbing a hill in the herringbone-fashion.

THE HALF-STAIRWAY STEP—
AN EASY WAY TO CLIMB

In a previous lesson, I told you how to climb straight up the fall line of a slope by using either the herringbone or the sidestep. To herringbone, you spread apart the fronts of the skis and walk up, splay-footed as a duck, making the inner edges of your skis bite into the snow. The sidestep, I explained, was done by standing sideways to the falling line and moving up laterally, very much as if you were standing sideways on a staircase and going up by moving to the side—which is why this method is sometimes called the stairway step.

In this lesson, I wish to show you the half-stairway step—so called, because you move forward and sideways at the same time. All the while, you remain in a position facing relatively square (or at 90 degrees) to the fall line. As you take a step forward, also move the ski sideways, before putting it down. Simple, isn't it? This method is less tiring than the other two because you don't have to lift each ski as much. When climbing by this method—just as with either of the other two—it is very important to make the uphill edges of the skis get a firm grip on the snow. And the harder the snow, the harder you must slam those edges into it. Which reminds me—are your edges really sharp enough to make climbing (and turning) as easy as it should be? If not, better have them sharpened, or do it yourself.

THIS IS THE SNOWPLOW

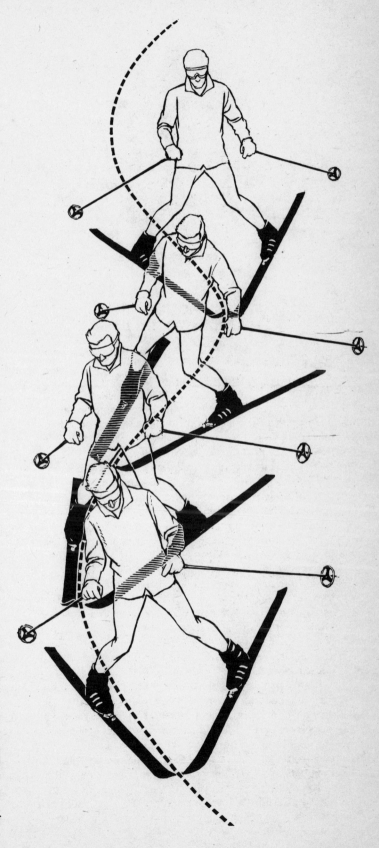

In this illustration you see me doing what is best described as a ''neutral'' way of making linked snowplow turns. The sequence of events starts from the snowplow position, such as the one described for you in a previous lesson. Note that my body is kept comfortably centered between the skis, that my weight rests relatively flat-footed along the entire sole of each foot, and that I bend slightly forward at the waist to maintain balance. Now, follow me down the hill. I begin to turn by pushing both knees forward and in toward the center of my intended turn—that's to my right. If the slope isn't too steep, my skis will turn to the right. As I begin to turn off the fall line, my weight gradually transfers automatically to my left ski (the one on the outside of the turn). I can increase the turning rate by leaning over that outside ski, which adds more weight to it, and by increasing the bite of its inside edge.

To turn to the left, I push both knees forward and in toward the imaginary center of a turn to the left. This gradually brings me into the fall line again and right off it, if I keep up the twisting action. As before, I can speed up the rate of the turn by leaning out over my outside ski—once that ski has begun to point toward the new direction—while simultaneously pushing my outside knee more forward and toward the inside of the turn.

Just about all experts of ski instruction agree that every skier must learn to snowplow at some relatively early stage of development, if for no other reason than to have a means of slowing down without changing direction. Agreement is less uniform regarding the snowplow turn, however.

The anti-snowplow-turners argue that snowplow habits are bad habits that have to be unlearned if the skier is to climb up the learning ladder. So why teach it in the first place? The pro-snowplow-turners argue that the turn's value lies in its ability to inspire confidence in the neophyte skier and to enable him to come down a gentle slope under control sooner than by any other means. However, even they admit that excessive snowplowing can develop bad habits, and they usually try to get the beginner out of this phase as fast as possible. I agree completely with this last practice. I see no reason why anyone should use snowplow turns, except in rare cases, after the first five to seven days of skiing.

WHEN SHOULD YOU
LEARN TO SKI?

I am often asked what's the ideal age for learning to ski? I answer quickly, when you want to, and I mean it. Shorter skis and better bindings to hold boots to skis have made our sport safer and easier to learn than ever before. I know many ski instructors who have given 70-year old students their first lessons. And I know others who have taught children three and four years old. And of course, thousands of people at all ages in between that range learn to have fun on skis every year.

Of course, if you've never been an athletic person, you will not progress as quickly as someone who is. For that reason, if you'd like your children to perhaps become a champion ski racer, then it is important to start young—certainly no older than eleven or twelve, and perhaps as young as four or five.

I believe the most important thing to learn first is that skiing out in the cold snow is a pleasant experience. Everyone should have fun at first, and should learn that as you improve you'll have even more fun. That way, it always seems worth the effort to improve, even if the cold does bother you a bit. Youngsters (and oldsters, too) must be dressed properly, so they get neither over-heated nor shivery cold.

I don't believe that children should be criticized when they are learning. They need encouragement. After all, they have to develop enough strength to handle their skis properly. For many kids, that is not until they reach 13 or 14 years of age. Those who ski regularly as youngsters may have the strength when they are between 10 and 12. In either case, that's the time when they can be taught to ski correctly—when they are strong enough, no matter what age. And I believe that only a very experienced ski instructor or coach can judge when that youngster is strong enough.

Maybe—you non-athletes—your time has come.

Not too many years ago, when you wanted to become a skier, you asked an expert for advice. He immediately had you stretch up your arm and advised you to buy a pair of skis that reached to your wrist. That was the basic rule and the reasoning behind it was simply that all good skiers—especially racers—used long skis, and therefore, so should you. If you stood, say, five-foot-eight in your stocking feet, then you should have skis almost seven feet long! No wonder skiing was difficult. No wonder you had to be an athlete to learn how to ski!

Thank goodness, those days are gone forever. To learn to ski, you don't have to be an athlete anymore, and you don't have to be as strong as an ox. Short skis (and plastic boots) have made the difference. Now, when you learn you can start out on skis about a yard long, and as you gain proficiency, you can progress to skis four feet long, then five feet, and if you do show signs of becoming an expert you can then move up to six-footers, or even seven footers. It's taken nearly seventy-five years for skiers to realize that anyone can learn to ski on short skis, and that only as you gain strength and confidence do you need longer ones. An added advantage is that short skis exert less leverage against your legs and can be moved almost as easily as your feet—so they are safer. You only need long skis if you ski fast, and you shouldn't ski fast if you aren't in top shape and skillful.

Consider this an invitation to join me in one of the world's most healthful sports, you non-athletes. I'll look for you on the slopes!

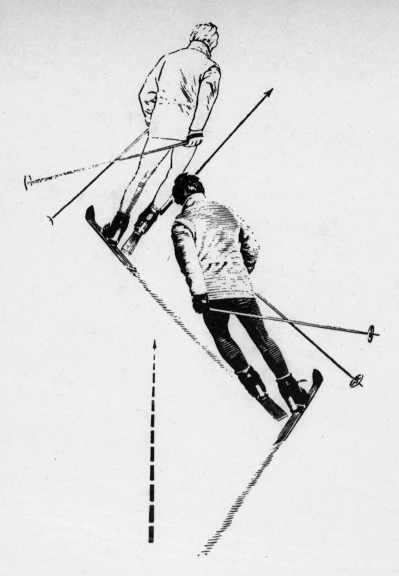

SKATING ON SKIS

I've won more than a few races by aggressively skating between gates to accelerate and get in the best position for the next turn. But skating is not just for competitors. For example, it can help give you a racer's confidence. Furthermore, a few fast skating steps at the start of your skiing day will warm you up and put you in a "forceful" frame of mind. I think this is important if your skiing is to improve.

By practicing skating, you will build a sense of balance and what we call *l'independence des jambes* (independence of the legs). This is the ability to ski on one leg independently of the other; a skill which is very important in modern skiing. Also you learn edge control and develop strength in the muscles and joints that control edging (ankles, knees and hips).

Here's how to skate on skis. As the sequence pictures indicate, I push off from the edged back ski and slide on the forward ski which is thrust out at an angle. But first, my upper body and hips twist and lean in the direction of the thrusting ski. You will notice that after the push off from the back ski, I quickly bring it alongside the forward foot, lifting its tip off the snow so it doesn't catch. All of my weight is now on the forward or sliding ski. The other ski remains in the air, but comes more or less parallel to the sliding ski as I start to lean and twist my body to the opposite side. Then I angle the new thrusting ski out and push off with the standing foot. What more can I tell you? It's skating, like on ice skates.

But I do have a few more hints: When first learning to skate don't use your poles . . . they may trip you. Later, learn to hold them parallel to the slope.

You might try rolling your ankle and knee inward just before the push off. By doing this, your back ski will edge and bite into the snow and give you a platform to push from. And be sure to bend your leg and lower hips so that you can push off with enthusiasm and get a nice long glide on the front foot.

After you can skate going straight ahead, try turning to one side . . . it's a good way to change direction. Then try skating when you are going down a moderate slope and also try the skating turn. *Magnifique!* You are on your way to doing a racer's skating-step turn. A little more practice and you might get to be an Olympic Champion.

THE KICK TURN

I want to show you how to make a kick turn. In France, we say *une conversion*. Experienced skiers do this turn without giving it a thought, but even an Olympic Champion like me at some time "way back when" had to cautiously try this for the first time. It's a snappy little maneuver . . . you're standing facing in one direction . . . zip, zip, you're facing the other direction. When you first learn you'll probably do it a few times just for the fun of it.

More than a fun thing, it's very useful when you're climbing up a slope diagonally using a half side step (I showed you this in an earlier lesson). When you reach the side of the slope you can do a kick turn and continue up in the opposite diagonal direction. When I'm inspecting a slalom course before a race and walking up and down to memorize the placement of the gates (the flags), I do many kick turns of this type. Also, kick turns can be useful in getting you down if you find you are over your head on a slope, if its steepness or conditions make you feel you can't do a moving turn. Take a slow traverse across the slope over to the side, stop, do a kick turn; traverse to the other side, kick turn, etc. It'll get you down safely.

Now here's how to do it. Stand with your skis heading across the hill, neither heading up nor down. Make sure that you have a steady "platform" before you start. In the illustrations, I'm going to kick with my left foot (shaded). This would be the downhill ski on a slope. In the first drawing, I have all my weight on my right foot while sliding the kicking foot back and forth a bit to "get the feel" for the movement. You do the same, and when you feel that you have the balance mastered, start your kick with a little backward "wind up" (see #2) and kick your whole leg up, waist high. At the same time bend your foot back a bit (the opposite of pointing your toe) so that the heel of the ski comes to rest on the snow by the tip of the other ski. If you don't get it up that far, you can't complete the rest of the turn properly. Now, using the heel of the ski as a pivot point, flop the tip of the ski out to the side and down flat next to the other ski as you see me doing in #3 and #4. You'll note that I have the ski pole on that side out of the way, back behind me, and that my body has turned half way. *Voilà!* You are now in what ballet dancers call "fifth position."

Complete the turn by putting your weight on the kicking foot while bringing the other one around . . . don't get it caught on that pole behind you. It helps to keep the feet and legs close as you bring the ski around. Your body and the right hand ski pole turn the rest of the way along with the turning ski (#5). When you finish up, you're facing the other way (#6). Practice this a few times . . . I'm sure it will become easy for you.

AN ENERGY SAVING TIP

In my last lesson I gave you pointers on how to perform the sidehill kickturn without losing your balance. Now, I would like to show you a little act which will make all your kickturns easier. In the illustration, I have already kicked around my first ski and am now bringing around the other. The dotted line shows where it will come to rest. For some reason, when most skiers bring around the second ski, they do so awkwardly, as if trying to lift the leg over a picket fence. Actually the legs and feet can be kept comfortably close together, which saves on a lot of expended energy, *if* a little effort is used to pick up the front of that second ski. All you have to do to get that second ski around is to lift up on the front of your foot, and the ski will swing around practically of its own accord. Try it.

THE SIDEHILL KICKTURN

This lesson deals with a variation of a very handy maneuver—the kickturn. I have already taught you that the kickturn is normally used to change direction quickly on flat terrain. Either foot and ski can be "kicked" around first. However, when doing a sidehill kickturn, (on a slope, of course, hence the name) only the lower ski can be safely kicked first. You can see from the illustration that as the lower ski is kicked around, you are in a precarious position. If your upper ski slipped forward, backward, or sideways, you could take an awkward, leg-tangled tumble. To guard against this take the following precautions: 1) Stand across the slope so that the skis will not move forward or backward of their own volition. 2) Stamp your upper ski firmly in place. 3) Place your ski poles behind you, as I have done. 4) When you kick that lower ski around, be conscious of getting a constant, firm, tripod support from the two poles and your upper leg and ski. 5) Once the lower ski has been kicked around into its new position, be very sure to place it directly across the slope so it will not move when you shift your weight to it and bring around the other ski. Do not move your ski poles until you've brought around both skis. Don't try this complete maneuver until you've mastered it first on the flats, then on gentle slopes.

TIPS ON TRAVERSING

It always amazes me to see how many self-taught skiers don't know how to traverse correctly. Traversing is simply a matter of skiing across a hill or, as instructors say, across the fall line. It's one of the first and best ways a learning skier has to control speed. When you ski down the fall line—schuss—you go fast. When you traverse you can pick any angle you want and so ski across the fall line at any speed you want. In fact, when your skis are on their uphill edges and at right angles to the fall line (that imaginary line which follows the downhill path a slow-moving ball would take), you will not move. Point your skis down the hill a few degrees and you can traverse at a slow, comfortable pace.

There is a proper way to stand on your skis for traversing, and it is important, for after all—even when you know how to make beautiful parallel christies, every one of those turns has to come to an end with a traverse, no matter how momentary. That moment will also be the time when you launch into your next christie, so if your body is not in a correct position at the outset of the turn, you will have a difficult time making your next turn.

Take a good look at me in this illustration. I am traversing a steep slope with the hill to my left and the valley to my right. Notice that the uphill edges of my skis are cutting a firm platform, which makes them go in the direction in which they point. One of the basic principles of good skiing is to keep body movements and positions symmetrical—the same on both sides. Because of the hill, note that my left foot is higher than my right. As far as that goes, everything on my left is similarly higher. In fact, a line drawn between my toes would be parallel to a line drawn through my knees, my hips and my shoulders. This position is what ski instructors call angulation. By rolling my knees and ankles toward or away from the mountain, I can make my skis edge more or less depending on the grip that I feel I need for ice or soft snow, and for the pitch of the slope.

I should also add that if I do push my knees toward the slope, my shoulders will tip slightly downhill increasing the amount of angulation. This helps me to keep slightly more weight on my lower ski. And that's an advantage when it comes to holding my direction while traversing.

SKID IT

When you find yourself on a steep slope, quivering in your boots, you will ease your mind if you remember that, after all, you don't have to go straight, or go across, or make turns down the run. You can always sideslip, or skid down. Sideslipping, because the full length of your edges can be used to brake your descent, allows you to go fast or slow, at your discretion. If you decrease the angle the bottoms of the skis make with the slope, the edges will lose their grip and you can ski sideways. Release the edge a considerable amount and you will skid fast, just a bit and you sideslip gradually. Not only is skidding a valuable, practical maneuver, it is excellent practice for learning parallel christies. When you realize that 80 to 90 percent of a parallel christie is a controlled sideslip, then you'll know why I say, skid it.

THE STEADY STANCE

It has been said, with good reason, that skiing is a game of balance. Part of the object in coming down a mountain is to do so without falling down. I believe anyone who can walk, run, and especially dance, has enough natural sense of balance to become a good skier. But you must learn certain things which make it easier to stay in balance. The most important of these is knowing the correct way to stand on skis.

Look at the illustration. See how I sort of slump. My knees are pushed forward so that I have a flexible bend at the ankles, and at the knees. And, very important, note that my shoulders are slightly rounded and that I have a slight bend at the waist. This over-all position makes it easy for me to keep my weight resting on the soles of my feet, with most of it pressing against the ball of each foot, where it should be most of the time. By keeping my shoulders forward the way I do—*never* letting them go furthur back than to where the illustration shows—I make sure that at least I will never be knocked over backwards, the way most learners fall. I may bend further forward at the waist, but not further backward. Not even to the point where I would be standing with my back almost upright. Remember to try this steady stance, and I am sure you will find your balance suddenly becomes *fantastique*.

FACTS ABOUT THE FALL LINE

As a skier, you'll fall now and then, of course. It's part of the sport. I, too, went through my apprenticeship and fell just like everybody else. But after years of experience, you will develop a remarkable resistance to falling, just as I did. The story of falling is a long one, and it will have to wait for another time because I now want to tell you about the fall line.

If you are a *débutante*—a newcomer—to skiing, you may think the fall line has something to do with the place where you fall. In a way, it does, but the relationship is only coincidental. The fall line is actually an idea—a handy way for skiers to describe their orientation on a slope. To put it another way, the fall line is an imaginary line which a ball would follow if it were allowed to roll

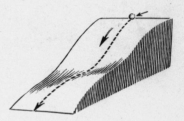

slowly downhill. In French we call this line *la ligne del la plus grande pente*—the line of the greatest pitch. It could also be called the line of least resistance or the line of fastest descent.

The illustration shows me just about to ski into the fall line. Since I'm making a turn (a parallel christie in this instance), no sooner will I ski into the fall line than I will ski off it to complete the turn. Skiing straight down the fall line is called schussing; skiing across it is called traversing. If you ski straight down a slope, making wiggle-like turns, you are said to be skiing close to the fall line, as in Wedeln.

It is important to recognize the fall line for several reasons: For one, if you want to slow down, you have to turn off the fall line or into the hill. For another, if you want to gain speed, you turn downhill or into the fall line. Another reason—once you understand the phrases about the fall line, communication with your fellow skiers will be much easier.

Oh, I almost forgot . . . about the relationship of the fall line to the place where you fall. As I mentioned, whenever you turn into the fall line, you'll pick up speed. That is the natural expectancy of any good skier. But when you are learning—and that's so long ago for me that I have almost forgotten about it—you may suffer a moment of anxiety as your skis slide faster and faster. So what do you do? Fall down. Where? Coincidentally, on the fall line!

ANKLE ACTION AND EDGE CONTROL

In this illustration, I am standing in a very uncharacteristic position for a racer. As every skier knows, it's the snowplow position—a position for braking, for slowing down. And that's the last thing a competitor wants to do. I am showing it to you because a good skier must learn how to use his ankle joints in a way not done in other sports.

You can practice this way by doing just what I am doing—bending my ankles outward, then pulling them back toward each other. This wrist-like action of the ankles is a skier's fine tuning instrument for controlling the play of the edges on the snow. The movement needed is only a slight amount—modern ski boots see to that—but it is very important to precisely control that amount. If you bend the ankle outward too much or too fast, your skis may skid out of control. If you don't bend enough, the edges will dig in and prevent you from skiing smoothly. Practice while standing still, as shown in the illustration, or while moving slowly downhill. Who knows? The strength and control you develop might help you, too, to become an Olympic champion. *C'est possible!*

SOME FACTS FOR YOUR SKIING SAFETY

Oooooooo! Someone is taking a dive into the powder. But then, so what? We all fall every so often and amazingly enough seldom suffer more than a blow to our dignity. But speaking very frankly, broken legs still do occur, even with the sophisticated release bindings which many of use use. And a broken leg is something everyone can do without. I believe the number of such injuries could be reduced sharply if every skier took the time to regularly check out his equipment. Here are some simple directions to follow, both when buying bindings and when regularly checking them.

1. Don't buy cheap bindings. Only the best ones can be expected to operate constantly.

2. The ski boot is part of the safety-release system. Not all boots work with all bindings, unless some minor modifications to either the boots or the bindings are made. Only a knowledgeable specialist knows these things. Be sure you deal with a store that knows what they are doing. How can you be sure? You can't be positive about that, but if the store uses a mechanical testing device to check for equal release to the right and left, and has you pull the boots free from the bindings at the heel, then you have reasonable assurance the shop knows what it's doing.

3. MOST IMPORTANT. If the binding needs it, insist that the store install a good quality, thick, anti-friction device under the ball of the foot. This is to overcome the friction that builds up between boot sole and ski, which might prevent the toe unit of the binding from operating. Mechanical anti-friction devices work even better than Teflon pads.

4. Because the bindings have to be adjusted to your boots, and because boot soles are not always exactly the same length, mark your skis LEFT and RIGHT to be sure of the correct boot and binding combination.

5. Spray boots and bindings with silicone every few weeks, to cut down on friction.

6. Always check the settings of the binding to be sure nothing has changed their correctness.

THIS IS CROSS COUNTRY SKIING

Everywhere in the world of winter sports, a new sport called cross-country skiing is taking hold. It's a new craze, new that is, everywhere except in Scandinavia, Finland, and parts of Russia, where the activity has been a necessary form of transportation in daily winter rural life for centuries. For the last 100 years or so—ever since the people of those countries were able to enjoy some leisure time—whole families have gone for a day's outing. Today, in the Scandinavian countries in particular, you find families out touring for weekends or longer periods, with the infants of the family being towed along in a small, lightweight sled (called a *pulka*) or snuggly tucked into a special back-mounted pack-frame.

Cross-country skiing can be as relaxing or as strenuous as you want to make it. Of course, since you must rely on your own muscle power—and not mechanical ski lifts—to get you uphill, your gear must be very light. The task of climbing uphill is made easy by the use of special waxes which, when properly applied, allow the skis to glide forward effortlessly, but prevent them from slipping back.

This variety of skiing is certainly not as thrilling as its mate, ski jumping, nor as exciting as the Alpine variety of down-mountain skiing which most skiers here are familiar with. But it does have its compensations. For one thing, cross-country skiing equipment is far less expensive—everything you need to get started can be bought cheaply. And another plus—you need not spend money for ski-lift tickets. Aside from these savings, the real pleasures come from being able to go some place—to move over hill and dale—and from the satisfaction always accompanying large-muscle activity. You actually feel good after an easy run on your cross-country skis.

Of course, another of the big appeals to the increasing number of cross-country skiers is the aesthetic experience. You can get away from crowds and truly enjoy the peace and quiet of snow gently falling on fir trees, or the sight of a snowshoe rabbit scampering through the bush. It would be easy for me to write much more about such things, but it would be much better for you if you were to try this delightful sport for yourself.

A SKIER'S SAFETY CODE

Every year more and more skiers are using the ski slopes. This means that as the slopes become more crowded, we skiers have to develop certain habits of safety to avoid collisions with each other. These habits need not be very complicated, for after all, skiing down a crowded ski slope is something like driving down a crowded highway. Common sense should prevail.

When the slopes are full of skiers, you must learn to ski defensively, keeping a wary eye out for the other guy. You mustn't go too fast, because at high speed you cannot always change your direction fast enough to avoid a collision. It might interest you to know that in some ski stations in Europe, there are course policemen who give citations to reckless or dangerously speeding skiers, who then have to appear in court to pay a fine. To try to avoid that kind of a situation over here, I've put together a few basic common sense rules.

1. Never ski so fast that you cannot stop in time to avoid another skier or obstacle.

2. Look behind you occasionally to be sure you are not moving on a converging path with another skier.

3. Always try to judge or anticipate the direction of the skiers ahead of you before overtaking them.

4. Never stop in the middle of a crowded run, just as you would never stop in the middle of the road when driving on a crowded highway.

5. Always, I repeat, always look above you before shoving off from your starting place to be sure you are not going to move right into the path of an oncoming skier.

I'm sure you could add some rules of your own to this code, and I hope you do. And I also hope you'll encourage your friends to do likewise. We'll all have more safe fun that way.

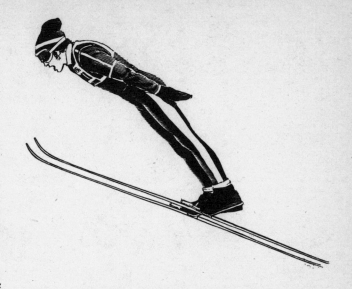

THIS IS NORDIC SKIING

Now, I'd like to tell you about another exciting phase of our sport, and that's Nordic Skiing, so-called because it was begun by the Norsemen many hundreds of years ago. In fact, a rock carving depicting a skier out hunting has been found in Norway, and it is said to have been done at least 2,000 years ago. Also, an actual ski tip was found in a Swedish peat-bog not too long ago, and scientists place its age at close to 4,000 years.

Through the intervening centuries, skis were used for transportation in almost all the northern parts of Europe and Asia, but especially in Scandinavia. Even today, in winter, Laplanders still tend to their herds of reindeer by moving about on their long, thin skis. The Norwegians, Swedes, and Finns have fought many a military battle in the wintertime—on skis. Today, the largest ski race in the world, the Vasaloppet, is held in Sweden each year to honor the successful victories of King Gustavus Vasa in the winter of 1519. That race is more than 50 miles long, over a lot of rolling terrain, and the winners run it in less than 7½ hours. It is one of the world's most grueling ski races. In spite of that, more than 8,000 racers take part in it every year. That gives you an idea as to just how popular Nordic skiing is in some parts of the world.

Despite its popularity, Nordic skiing did not become a sport until the last half of the 19th century, when people began to have a little leisure time in winter. During those days, in the gentle mountains near Telemark, not far from Oslo, Norway, ski races were held across country, and simple jumping competitions became popular—all very humble beginnings for Nordic skiing which, in 1924, became a part of the Olympic Winter Games, held in Chamonix, France.

THIS IS SKI JUMPING

Ski jumping is a very specialized sport. Special jumps have to be built on specially prepared hills. The jump consists of a high scaffold—sometimes nearly 200 feet high—to provide the inrun slope and the take-off for the jumpers. The inrun is often as steep as 40 degrees at the top. Then it must have a smooth transition to the take-off point so the jumpers won't be thrown off balance before leaping off. The take-off is usually horizontal, and anywhere from eight to twenty feet high. The landing hill consists of a gently sloping brow, for 100 or more feet, followed by the actual landing area which is a very steeply inclined section pitched at 37 degrees. At what is called the critical point, the transition to the flat outrun begins. That point is critical because the slope becomes less and less steep, consequently the jumpers would land here with an ever-increasing force.

Ski jumpers use very special skis. They are seven to eight feet long and half again as wide (over four inches) as any of the skis used for Alpine skiing. These skis weigh almost twenty pounds per pair. Since a ski jumper has to take off the lip at something close to 60 mph, moving in a perfectly straight line, each ski has three or four deep, sharply edged grooves running almost the entire length of the ski's bottom to provide the needed directional stability.

As you can see in the illustration, the ski jumper has to learn to shape his body over his skis so that he assumes a shape like the cross section of the wing of an airplane. This airfoil shape actually creates lift, and to a large extent the distance the jumper will cover is determined by the perfection of this position.

In Olympic competition, two sizes of jumping hills are used—a 70-meter and a 90-meter—and Olympic distance records stand at about 240 feet off the small hill and 300 feet off the big hill. However, the world's distance record is an almost unbelievable 514 feet. This was achieved in a very specialized form of jumping called "ski flying." There are only six jumping hills in the world specially constructed for leaps of more than 500 feet, and one of these is on the North American continent at Copper Peak, Michigan.

EQUIPMENT FOR CROSS COUNTRY SKIING

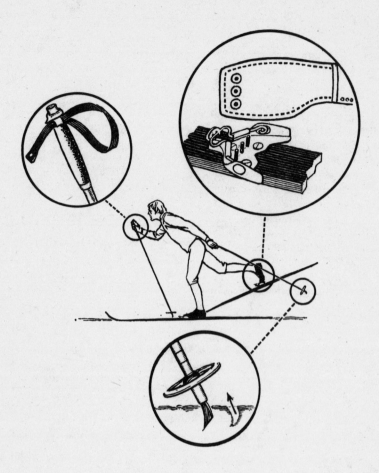

The ancient sport and mode of transportation called cross country (or X-C) skiing is now rapidly gaining in popularity. Gaining, perhaps because the sport seems less dangerous than pitting yourself against gravity and a mountain, as in "ski-lift" or Alpine skiing. Also, people everywhere want to get away from crowds, to be on their own again. Or perhaps the sudden rapid increase in interest is because you don't need to spend money on lift tickets, and because you can buy everything you need for X-C skiing for under $100.

The cost is low because X-C equipment is relatively easy to manufacture. The skis, for example, are usually made of laminated hardwoods such as birch and ash. Though they are made to be longer than normal Alpine skis, they are often less than two inches wide and without steel edges. This makes them very light indeed—some weigh barely two pounds per pair.

The bindings are also extremely light—a matter of ounces—since all they have to do is clamp the front of the boot to the ski. The ski boot heel must be free to lift off the ski unimpeded so that you—like a runner—can make long graceful strides. Once you learn this—the kick and glide, it's called— you go zipping over flat stretches of snow at better than 20 mph and with very little effort.

Cross country ski boots are usually of leather and are cut very low—almost like a track shoe. Instead of spikes on them, however, they may have holes in the sole at the toe to accept pins which stick up from the binding, thus assuring a good firm grip between ski and boot. The boots often weigh less than street shoes.

The last remaining piece of specialized equipment for the X-C skier are the ski poles. These usually extend to the height of your shoulders, as opposed to those which I would use for slalom, which only reach to my elbow. The poles are often of special lightweight bamboo or aluminum, with a simple cork grip and leather strap for the wrist. The steel point of the pole is curved forward so that it slips easily out of the snow as you go gliding past.

Cross country skiing is a lot of fun. You should try it soon.

PACKING FOR YOUR SKI TRIP

When you have gone through all the effort of getting to a ski area, you want to be sure you haven't forgotten to bring something that you are going to need. It's easy to overlook an item such as ski gloves or boots in the last minute rush to get off. So why don't you sit down and make a checklist of the things you'll need? If you like, you can use my checklist as a guide.

As you see, my check list is in three sections: "Musts" which you will need on any trip . . . day, weekend, week or longer. "Handy" are those items which are good to have, but not essential. "Extras" are the things which you may or may not want or need depending on where you are staying, how long you'll stay and what you plan to do. Some of these "Extra" items would be the kind of thing you'd want to consider when you are taking a ski vacation of a few days or more.

Before you go on your first trip of the season, check off the items which you already have, and then you'll know what you need to get. It will help you avoid those last minute lapses of memory.

MUSTS	HANDY	EXTRAS
Skis	Additional Sweaters	Pajamas, Robe, Slippers
Poles	Lightweight Parka	Extra Apparel
Wax	Warm-up Suit, Pants	Pant Suit, Culottes,
Parka	Fanny Pack, Belt Pouch	Long Skirt
Sweater	Camera, Film	(for girls);
Turtleneck Shirt	Foam Padding for Boots	Flannel Slacks, Blazer
Hat/Headband	Nylon Windshirt	or Sport Jacket,
Goggles/Glasses with	Skier's Release Check	Silk T-Necks for
yellow and green lenses	Extra-Stretch Pants	men
Lip and Sun Cream	After-Ski Sweater or	Dress Shoes
Boots on Boot Tree	T-neck	Dress-Up Apres-Ski
Ski Lock	Knickers, Knee Socks	Boots
Ski Ties or Carrier	Face Mask	Jacket, Coat, Cape
Stretch Pants	Additional Underwear,	Gloves
Thermal Underwear	T-necks, Glove Liners	Handbag or Ski Pouch
Socks—Heavy, Light	Edge File, Base Repair	Tie or Ascot
Mittens/Gloves	Kit	
After-Ski Boots		
Binding Tool, Silicone		
Spray		
Tissues, Band-Aids,		
Aspirin, Sewing Kit		

KEEP IN SHAPE DURING THOSE LONG, SNOWLESS MONTHS

Many people ski to keep in shape. But me, I keep in shape to ski. In my home town of Val d'Isere in the French Alps, I can ski 12 months of the year—If I want to. I don't because there is such a thing as getting stale—of having too much of a good thing.

So, to keep in shape during those few months when I hardly ski, I take active part in sports which require a lot of action. I play tennis, partly because it develops fast reflexes, good timing, and balance. It keeps the trunk and arms in good shape. I do a lot of bicycling on the roads around home because the excercise develops strong legs and a flexible back. And I run a lot, uphill and down, principally to develop my endurance. I also lift weights to build up certain muscles needed for competition skiing.

You should make plans to take up a sport which will help you to improve or maintain your physical condition. This applies even if you are a "Sunday skier." For physical fitness will allow you to lead a longer, healthier, more pleasurable life and will have a positive effect on virtually all aspects of your daily existence. Choose activities which build strength, coordination and endurance, but most importantly, ones that you enjoy so that you will look forward to rather than dread the next session. Follow this advice and voila! At the start of the season you will be in fantastic condition.

2-The Intermediate Skier

A KEY TO SKIING— SIDESLIPPING

I once heard a debutant—a beginner—speak of skiing as having two kinds of turns. He said, "There are grinders and there are swishers, and I'm tired of grinding my way down. I want to learn to come down and go swish-swish-swish, like the better skiers." He was talking about the difference between the slow turns which many learners use—where the strength of the legs forces and steers the skis around—and the smooth, graceful turns, called christies, which experts use to make their skis skid around effortlessly.

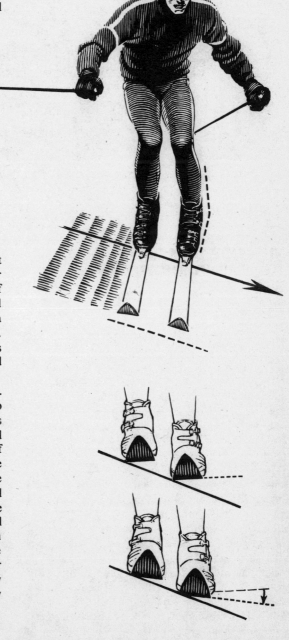

It takes finesse rather than strength to make perfect christies. Speaking very simply, what you do is turn your skis at an angle to your direction of travel, and get yourself started into a skid. Then you control the edges of your skid to control how much and how fast you turn. A christie is a skidded turn, or as instructors call it, a sideslipping turn. Since more than three-quarters of the turn involves sideslipping, you can see why it is important to understand how to control the edges of your skis.

In the large drawing you see me practicing sideslipping. I am not turning—I am just allowing myself to slip sideways down the hill—down the fall line, as instructors say. The small sketches show how I move my knees and ankles away from the hill to decrease the angle the soles of my skis make with the snow. In the upper sketch, where my skis are "edged," I travel in the direction in which the skis point. But in the lower one, where I have "released my edges," I skid sideways. This is where the finesse comes in. I must not release the edges too much, or I will fall over sideways, downhill. And if I don't release them enough, I won't be able to make my skis sideslip. I hope you won't think I am a Simon Legree if I say you had better practice sideslipping—facing in each direction—for nearly ten hours, over a period of several days, before you really say you know how to do it.

PRACTICE SIDESLIPPING FOR SKIING KNOW-HOW

Would you like to know one of the real secrets of skiing? If so, study the illustration carefully. Here, you see three drawings of me skiing across the hill. In a way, I am traversing or, as your ski instructor would say, I am skiing across the fall line. However, I'm not actually moving exactly in the direction my skis point. Instead I am sliding both forward and sidewards at the same time. Technically, you would say I am sideslipping diagonally. There are many variations of sideslipping and each one is handy—worthwhile practicing. Also the turns which good skiers use (christies) basically consist of sideslipping. It is important to learn.

Sideslipping is skidding. Follow me as I demonstrate. First I start moving across the hill. My body is in the proper traversing position to insure that my skis cut a clean, shelf-like track in the snow. Your legs and feet do not have to be as close together as mine are. Sometimes I hold them very close because it looks good, but it is harder to keep balanced. On the other hand, any maneuver on skis, sideslipping included, becomes awkward when your feet become separated by more than eight inches. In the middle figure, I have rolled my knees and ankles away from the hill. That movement is called releasing the edges. Some people call it flattening the skis, but for sideslipping you don't ever actually flatten the skis on the snow. They must always be on their uphill edges, at least slightly. The lower ankle must also bend away from the slope (small diagram) to make the release of the edges even easier. I like to think of the work which the knees and ankles do in sideslipping this way: the knees are the gross adjusters, while the ankles are the fine tuners. In the last figure, you'll see that I have re-edged my skis by bringing my knees back toward the slope and allowing my shoulders to tilt slightly toward the valley—all movements which lead me back on to a new traverse.

At first the sensation of sliding sideways feels unusual. Most people release the edges too fast—the skis then slip away quickly, and you are left behind them, leaning into the hill. That either makes the skis re-edge or slip right out from under you. Release the edges s-l-o-w-l-y, and as you feel the skis start to slip out from under you, also make your body move sideways by leaning in the same direction.

Here is a good exercise to do. Traverse a hard-pack slope as I am doing in the illustration. Then release the edges and re-edge the skis every few seconds. Many a certified ski instructor has told me that all skiers could really improve their slope technique, if they'd just practice sideslipping regularly. To that I would add—get your practice under the supervision of a certified instructor. You'll be handsomely rewarded in terms of faster progress and more fun.

POWER FROM THE POLES

How long are your poles? Do they reach to your waist, or to your armpits? How long should they be? Well, that all depends on what you want to use them for. I like to get power from mine—pushing power—so I use poles a little on the long end of the range. Let me explain.

A pole that reaches to your waist is a short one. Poles that reach to your armpits are long ones. I like mine to reach somewhere between these extremes. (To measure the poles, stand them up alongside you while standing on a hard floor.) I don't like poles longer than 75 percent of my height nor shorter than 70 percent. I believe that to be the comfortable range for just almost everybody. Anything more or less than that is extreme.

Choose the shorter poles if you intend to race slalom or ski hard and fast in the moguls. Choose something in between if you are an average skier who doesn't go to extremes. And choose a lenght around 75 percent of your height if you are a giant slalom racer who wants a little extra pushing power that comes from the extra length. But be prepared to work harder with your arms when skiing slalom or the moguls for the extra length makes quick arm movements a bit slower and a bit more awkward.

SETTING THE EDGES

In the last two lessons, I told about sideslipping—the art of letting your skis slip sideways without losing your balance. I mentioned how important it was to learn *les nuances*—the subtleties—of this art by moving the knees and ankles sideways just the right amount. These leg movements, transmitted through your boots, change the angle the bottom of the skis make with the snow, allowing you to skid fast or slow. I mentioned that sideslipping was mainly a matter of finesse rather than strength, and that more than three-fourths of a christie—those great-feeling, swooshing turns which experts use—is a matter of sideslipping.

Now, I want to tell you about a very specific sideslipping exercise which will help you develop the ability to end a christie very quickly, to either stop on a dime or start a turn in the other direction *tout de suite*. The exercise is called setting the edges. The upper figure in the illustration, the one to the right, shows that I am letting myself skid sideways down the slope. In the lower figure, see how I have moved my knees toward the hill to make the edges of the skis bite the slope. The instant I do that, the skis and I start moving forward again. With practice, you can set your edges this way when you want to stop skidding in a christie. To master the technique, choose a smooth, packed slope steep enough for easy sideslipping. Move your knees and ankles away from the hill just enough to start skidding. Skid sideways a foot or so, then set the edges. Repeat. Repeat again. To develop even more precision, learn to flex your legs as you skid, so that at the instant you push your knees sideways, you can also straighten the legs, somewhat as if you were trying to push the edges into the snow. This assures the edges will bite firmly.

In the illustration you can see how I get my pushing power. Just be sure that when you stretch forward to plant your poles you have them slanted backward slightly. That way, the instant the points take hold in the snow you can first pull yourself forward and then push yourself ahead. I think I've won a few races just because I knew when and how to push, and my poles were long enough to give me the power. I'd recommend you buy yours just a bit on the long side. They can always be cut down to your preferred length—once you find it.

THIS IS SCHUSSING

For me, there's a real challenge, a special thrill, in going straight down a ski slope. You don't make any turns, you just go all out in a sort of power dive. Skiers call this schussing. It's a German word and it is quite appropriate for it means to shoot.

Of course, schussing a slope can be dangerous, but only for the foolhardy. And I would call foolhardy anybody who exceeds his capabilities by too much. For those who go about schussing with care and consideration rewards are there in terms of improved skills, greater confidence and thrills.

For me, schussing is easiest and safest when I keep my feet and skis apart about the same width as my hips. When I go really fast—over 45 miles per hour—I don't try to ski with perfect form. Then I am too busy concentrating on balance, keeping my weight as evenly distributed as possible on each foot. My ankles, knees and waist bend and unbend constantly, compensating for changes in snow and terrain.

As a beginner, learn to schuss on very gentle slopes even if you go no faster than 5 miles per hour. Look for obstacle-free slopes which have a flat runout so you will come to a natural stop. Stand on your skis in much the same fashion you see me doing here.

If you're an intermediate, seek out a similar slope. Of course, it should be pitched at a steeper angle.

To become an advanced or expert skier you must develop the confidence and ability to ski fast. Once you have mastered the basic christies, then by all means seek out places to practice fast skiing. An excellent place is at the bottom of a steep slope. First, practice schussing the last 10-20 yards of the slope. Then gradually work your way into starting higher and higher up-slope. I am sure this will enhance your skiing enjoyment enormously as you learn to enjoy the taste of more speed in your skiing.

THE FANNY PACK

This may come as a surprise to you, but it is true—I have always noticed how much better the average North American skier is in comparison to his European counterpart. Perhaps it is because in general your mountains have shorter vertical descents than our Alps do, so that you place more emphasis on how to turn and get a great deal of pleasure from this, while our people are more eager just to be able to get down the big mountains, to enjoy the magnificent vistas, and to get from one place to another.

But the skiers of the Alps make use of a handy gadget which I don't often see used on the ski slopes of this continent. That gadget is the fanny pack, a small, body-contouring, soft leather or plastic container which belts around your waist and sits across the top of your rump. These packs come in many sizes, shapes, and colors, and you can surely find one to suit your needs. Here is a list of the kinds of items you might want to safely tuck into a fanny pack—I say safely because even sunglasses in a good case are relatively safe from harm back there, nestled in the small of your back:

A touch-up file, for repairing annoying rock-bruises on your steel edges.

Sunglasses or goggles with interchangeable or different colored lenses—amber for flat light, grey, brown, or green for brilliant light.

Ski wax and a small scraper, for changing snow conditions.

Soft tissue for wiping goggles, or your nose.

A screw driver, small pliers, or a binding adjusting tool.

Extra cap, gloves, or even a windshirt.

A candy bar, or raisins, for quick energy.

Cosmetics and sun creams.

Whatever else of convenience which might save you a trip back to the base lodge or the distant parked car.

TAKING A LESSON

Skiing is so much fun, so absorbing, that it is easy to become complacent about your progress. It amazes me to look at a slope full of weekend skiers and note how much bad skiing goes on. It's not that I object to bad skiing, it's just that I know how much more fun skiing becomes when you know how to ski well. When you don't ski with the right techniques, you may have a terrible time on hard surfaces or on snow that is broken up or even on snow that is wonderfully deep.

There are two ways to learn the techniques for different or unusual snow conditions. First way (the hardest to learn), is to watch better skiers than yourself and try to imitate their movement. The other way is to take a lesson from a competent, certified ski instructor. If the instructor is good, you will learn a number of very helpful things even in just one lesson, though it is usually best to give your teacher a fair chance by taking at least 3 or 4 lessons.

I would urge you to take a group or class lesson first. There you will not only profit from the instruction given you but also from seeing and listening to the errors and corrections given to the others. If you have a peculiar or special problem which would be best corrected through an hour or two of concentrated effort, your instructor will recommend a private lesson. Though it may cost 2 or 3 times as much as a group lesson, the dividends to be earned in terms of more pleasure and safety could be worth far more than the cost.

In the illustration you see me leading down a couple of people who want to improve. I have instructed them to stay very close to me and to follow as exactly in my tracks as they can. This way, they can imitate my movements, almost without thinking of them and profit by my ability to choose the right (easiest) place to turn. An accomplished instructor will ask you to do just the same both in class and with private lessons. Do your best to follow closely when your turn comes.

CROSSING FROM FLAT SLOPE TO STEEP

If you are skiing on a relatively flat slope and come to a steeper one, you must learn to anticipate the sudden acceleration you'll experience. You do this by leaning forward before you get to the steeper pitch, no later than the time that your feet reach the crest of the drop-off. Keep your hands in front of your hips (this will help you keep your weight forward). If you don't anticipate in this way, your skis will go scooting out in front of you with their new found acceleration and you will fall backward on your *derriere*.

A similar situation arises when you go from slower snow to faster snow . . . such as from unpacked to packed snow or from "good" snow to ice. Again you must anticipate your scooting skis and lean forward before you reach the faster snow.

After you have completed the transition onto the steeper or faster slope, you can resume your original upright balanced position.

CROSSING FROM STEEP SLOPE TO FLAT

In my downhill racing days, I'd often reach speeds of 80 miles per hour or more. At speeds like that you have to anticipate transitions in terrain if you want to stay in one piece. But it's just as important for you or me when moving along at only 8 mph to look ahead to see what's coming up. Bumps, hollows, icy spots, soft spots . . . all kinds of things await the unwary; ready to take you by surprise. One of the changes of terrain which once gave me fits, ready or not, was the transition from a steep slope to a flat. As your skis go through the change of terrain, it feels like the body is being compressed and that you are about to be pitched forward onto your face. And believe me, that's just what can happen unless you train yourself to handle such situations.

When you are skiing from a steeper slope to a flatter one, you must learn to anticipate the transition. Your momentum will want to flatten you out and pitch you on your face since your skis will suddenly slow down more than your body does.

You can prepare for these forward forces by leaning back a bit just before the skis make the transition. Also, absorb these forward and downward forces by bending at your ankles, knees and waist. Compress downward, but don't collapse.

This rapid slowing down also occurs when you go from packed snow to loose, deep snow. You must anticipate the change before you get to it.

THE STEM CHRISTIE

The stem christie is not part of my regular repertoire. As far as I'm concerned it is a ski school maneuver—something which should be abandoned before the stemming movements become a habit almost impossible to correct.

A stem is a movement accomplished by using one leg and foot to separate the tails of the skis. A snowplow is sometimes called a double stem and a stem is sometimes called a half snow plow. In the illustration, you see me traversing a smooth-packed hill. Uphill is to my right. Note that my skis are parallel, my legs comfortably apart, and my body centered and squared directly over my skis. In the second illustration (from right to left), I have started to stem. The lower ski (my left) remains edged and on its traversing course. I have picked up the heel of my uphill ski and moved it away from the lower one in the classic uphill stemming manner. Notice that I have brought forward my lower pole. The stemming action places my uphill ski closer to the fall line that I am about to turn into. The third figure in the sequence shows me at the moment I'm about to jab my pole into the snow. The moment it is in the snow, I shift my weight to my stemmed ski and move my body to force around the heel of that ski.

In the final figure I have crossed the fall line. Note that I have now brought the inside ski of my turn alongside of and parallel to the outside ski of the turn. The stemming action is now over and the christie or skidding phase has begun. From here on, I merely sideslip around the rest of the turn as if I were making an uphill christie. In an earlier lesson, I explained how to move your weight and adjust the angles your edges make in the snow to control the skidding action.

The stem christie must be performed with enough speed to allow the skis to skid easily—that's somewhere between 10 and 15 miles per hour. There's no question about it—skiing becomes really fun once you learn to stem christie—so much fun that too many skiers forget that this is only part of the way up to great skiing. You will never enjoy the full benefits of control and thrills on skis until you discard the stem and become a parallel skier.

HOW YOU CAN DEVELOP CONFIDENCE

For me, of the three disciplines of Alpine skiing, downhill was the toughest to conquer. Because I was naturally *bien doué* (or, as you would call it, well endowed) with quick reflexes, slalom races were the easiest to win. And, because I worked hard to develop my strength, I was able to triumph in giant slalom events. But, developing my self-confidence was what finally enabled me to win an Olympic gold medal in the downhill.

You, too, *mon ami*, must become confident before you will enjoy the thrills of skiing. In the illustration, you see me airborne in a deep tuck position, streamlined to the wind. In a moment I will partially straighten up so I can bend deeply again the instant my skis come in contact with the snow. The timing of my movements must be exact. If I lose my nerve, even for a split second, my timing would be affected and I could take a bad fall. Believe me, I had to build up much confidence to sail off a bump at 100 kilometers an hour without losing my nerve.

It is a normal part of skiing for everyone, beginner to expert, to be accidentally launched into the air. To learn to enjoy the thrill without losing your nerve, take time to practice jumping. Beginners should learn to hop while sliding at 5 miles an hour. Intermediates should be able to sail comfortably off a one-foot high bump, going 10 miles an hour, and travel in the air for a ski length or two. Advanced skiers should be able to do much more than that.

Gradually, build up your confidence, never going off bumps which would be dangerous for a skier of your ability. Practice regularly, always challenging yourself by going just a bit faster, higher, and farther than the last time. Then, when you accidentally become airborne, you will not lose your nerve. Instead, you will enjoy the thrills more than ever.

HOW TO NEGOTIATE THE BUMPS

When you begin to ski you will probably spend all of your time on a smooth beginner's slope. This is good. A smooth slope lets you relax more because there are no bumps to throw you. You can let your skis run a little and get a safe taste of that speed I love so much.

However, when you leave the beginner's area you will find that most slopes have bumps. These can be small and frequent, giving you a "washboard" type of ride that rattles your teeth. Or they can be bigger, up to head-high bumps or moguls that can really give you a roller coaster effect and make you miserable . . . until you learn to handle them. Then they can be fun and exciting. So let's learn.

In the illustration you see me going through a series of moguls. See how my legs are extended in the hollow between the moguls and retracted on the crests. Also notice that while my skis follow the bumpy contour of the terrain, my head, neck and shoulders stay on a straight line moving down the slope. Actually I have "erased" the effect that the moguls would have had on me if I remained stiff-legged. In France we call this movement *avalement* (a-val MON), which means swallowing . . . you swallow the mogul by these retracting/extending leg movements.

Let's go through it step-by-step. You approach the bump in a normal, fairly erect stance. Don't bend forward from the waist before you get to it . . . that's a mistake. As your skis start climbing up the bump, let your legs retract under your body and start leaning forward from the waist, so that when you are at the crest you are in a crouched position, arms low and in front of the body. When you've passed the crest, consciously extend your legs back down into the hollow. This keeps your skis firmly on the snow and you get the control that you wouldn't have if your skis were flying off into space. At the bottom of the hollow you should again have the extended, almost erect stance. As the next bump comes along, again let your "landing gear retract" at the crest and let down on the other side. With practice, to get the timing of the bumps, you'll soon become adept. And what a thrilling new dimension you'll have added to your repertoire.

RIDING A SMALL BUMP

It is very likely that your first days of skiing were spent on carefully prepared nursery slopes. So much the better, since natural, unprepared slopes are full of bumps, hollows and rough snow. The care and attention which ski area people now give to slope grooming and snow conditioning have made skiing easier and safer for everyone. Before too long, however, every skier runs into bumps—big or small. Though you may not have realized it, the size of the bump makes a difference in how you ski it.

I'd like to tell you how to ride the small ones. By small, I mean bumps the size of moguls—those humps which build up on steep slopes. It seems that our skis push snow into piles and as more skiers follow, usually in the same tracks, the grooves get deeper and the bumps get higher.

When you ski into a bump, the first thing it does is slow down the speed of your skis and you then pitch forward. Avoid being thrown on your face in two ways. The first is to bend deeply at the ankles, knees and waist. The second is to anticipate the jerk forward by leaning back slightly, just before the slowing-down action begins.

In the illustration I am absorbing the shock of the bump by bending deeply. In a sense, the objective is to try to avoid disturbing your head and shoulders. You can see that mine stay at almost the same level, more or less parallel to the general downward direction of the slope, even though the bump protrudes upward at least several feet. There's a lot of weight concentrated in the shoulders,

so the less they are moved about, the less likely are you to disturb your balance. And since the head contains delicate organs of balance, the less it is moved about the keener is your sense of balance.

You'll notice that when I slide down the far side of the bump, I am on a rather steep slope. Therefore, since it is important for balance to keep the body over the skis, I must make an effort to lean forward more as my skis start down the steep side. You can see how I've let the up-side of the bump pitch my body forward, not too much, but just enough so that I am in the right position of forward lean as I get to the steeper down-side.

Now, that's lot of detail and you are not going to learn to ski over the bumps just by reading. You must get out and practice over easy bumps, learning to feel the stresses and strains, and learning to respond to them—with the proper timing. I can only give you a clue to what is proper timing, but you must learn for yourself how to adjust for every different condition. The clue is this—stand tallest in the hollows, crouch lowest on the crest. The speed of your movements going from high to low and back to normal again, must correspond to the speed at which you travel over the hump. That is, the faster you go, the faster your movements must be.

Don't expect to master bumps in a few easy practice sessions. But do keep at it. For me, next to skiing as fast as I can and skiing in the powder, skiing the bumps holds enormous excitement. It will for you, too.

JUMP BEFORE THE BUMP

Sometime along the way to becoming a good skier, you'll have to learn a little bit about ski jumping. At the very least, you'll have to get used to leaving the ground for a half-second or so, so as not to lose your composure when you accidentally ski off the edge of a steep mogul or mound. In the previous lesson, I told you how to jump and keep your balance, so now I'd like to tell you about another way to keep yourself standing when you encounter rough terrain. It's called pre-jumping.

Pre-jumping is just what it says—jumping before the bump. The idea is to lift off into the air before you get to the bump, sail over it, and land on smoother ground. The reason for this maneuver is sensible—when you pre-jump you can control your airborne height and distance, but when you sail off a bump, those two factors are uncertain quantities, and you might be thrown much higher and farther than would be prudent or safe.

To loft yourself into the air before your skis hit the bump is not too difficult—the movements are very much like those used to spring into the air while standing on the floor, for example. First, you lower your body position, and very quickly and powerfully you extend the legs. As soon as your skis leave the snow, pull the knees up toward your chest. Once the obstacle or bump has been cleared, lower the legs to prepare for a landing. And don't forget to flex the legs the instant the skis contact the snow, to insure a smooth landing. I'd advise you to practice on smooth, easy slopes first. Then, as you gain confidence and skill, try pre-jumping a small hump or other easy obstacle and gradually build up to where you can confidently and safely leap over the biggest of moguls and land on the steep downside of another one farther down the slope.

A TURN FOR MOGULS

In the previous lessons, I told you how to ski over bumps or moguls when going in a straight line. Now I'm going to show how to use moguls to make almost effortless parallel christies. The facts are that moguls help you to unweight, pivot your skis into the new direction, and make the proper change of your edges . . . things which are the guts of any parallel turn.

Here's how I do this mogul christie. I ride my skis to the mogul and as my tips pass the crest, I plant my pole near the top of the bump, comfortably off to the side. You can see the pole placement in the first figure. Also note that I've started to anticipate the direction of this approaching right turn by bringing my right shoulder and arm forward while letting my body tip slightly toward the fall line. These movements will make it easier to give turning power to the skis at the brief instant they are balanced on the crest of the mogul when their tips and tails are ever so slightly off the snow. At this pivot point, my skis will swivel easily because the only part touching the snow is a small area under my feet. As my feet pass over this point, I quickly move my knees to the inside of the turn, and twist my feet in the desired direction. This forces the skis to pivot and changes them to what will become the inside edges of the new turn.

The second figure shows that I've lowered my hips to absorb some of the jolt of the bump and to unweight my skis a little. This movement also slightly prolongs the brief period during which I can swivel my skis. Once the skis have turned, I then move my hips up and forward, as in the third figure, to cause the skis to regain full contact with the snow. They will now skid around easily to complete the christie and I'll control its radius by the amount of edging and steering I do with my knees and feet, just as in any christie, into the hill.

Practice this easy christie by actually stopping on top of a mogul and balancing yourself in the pivot position I've described. Plant your pole and support yourself on it. Then, in a smooth sequence, lower your hips, crank your feet and knees around, and tip forward a little with your upper body. Push off the pole, and . . . whoosh . . . pivot. Down and around you go. *Fantastique!*

HOW TO UNWEIGHT

Basically, skis want to go in a straight line on the snow. They are five to seven feet long, have a straight groove down the middle and steel edges that grip the snow. This gives them a kind of "one track mind." Therefore, for most turns, especially the christies, you have to get your weight off the skis so they can lose this tight grip on the snow and be steered into a new direction. This lightening of the skis is called unweighting.

I am doing a parallel christie in this illustration, using pronounced up-unweighting. If you are a beginner, you won't be doing this sort of turn right away, not with long skis anyway, though your instructor might let you try it with short (four-foot) ones. As illustrated, first I crouch down and set my edges to get ready to rebound upward. Then I spring up by quickly straightening my legs. This sudden "up" motion results in an unweighting of my skis . . . sometimes even lifting them from the snow. Once the skis are unweighted like this, I can turn them easily.

In most situations a moderate, but fast, "up" motion with the skis remaining on the snow allows enough time to get a parallel christie started. Note that in the second picture my knees are still slightly bent and my upper body

is inclined somewhat forward. I never straighten up all the way, because the amount of unweighting depends less on the amount of "up" than it does on the speed of execution. A small, but quick, explosive movement is what you should work for.

Another way to unweight is by a downward movement, done correctly by quickly pushing the knees forward and simultaneously dropping the hips. Though this method only gets weight off the skis for a fraction of a second, it's still long enough to loosen their grip so your turning power will take effect. Instructors differ in the emphasis they give to up- or down-unweighting in teaching people to ski. When I analyze films of myself, in a slalom course for instance, I see that I spring up when I've the time to, and drop down when the time is short.

There are times when you need hardly unweight at all, such as on icy snow where your skis can skid around easily, or on moguls which are easy to swivel around because of their shape. In these two situations, you will want to keep your skis down on the snow as much as possible to remain in control and to concentrate on suppressing any excessive unweighting movements. On the other hand, in deep snow, you will have to work to exaggerate the amount of unweighting.

FEELING FORWARD

You hear a lot of talk these days about sitting back on your skis. Fine. But sitting back at any time puts you in a precarious position—your skis can easily scoot ahead of you, leaving you sitting on the snow. If you want to sit back for special purposes, better practice first while you are not moving. In particular, you must practice how to get forward again, in a hurry. The illustration shows a good way to practice both these movements. Find a flat spot to stand on, where your skis will move neither forward nor backward. Then move into the positions you see me in here—first, with your weight forward, pressing on the ball of each foot, then sitting back. Move back and forth a dozen times. Repeat periodically. This exercise can help you to learn to tell what your body position is by the *feel* of the boots against your feet.

THIS IS A PARALLEL CHRISTIE

One of the great things about skiing is that it's a lot of fun, even if you are learning. But you can only begin to get the full measure of pleasure once you master the skill of the basic parallel christie. After that, the mountain is yours.

There are so many variations to this kind of turn that you can ski fast or slow, adapt your skiing to all types of snow and all types of terrain. When you really understand the subtle things your feet and legs have to do, your skis will take you safely through any number of obstacles.

Before giving you the key to making parallel christies, I would like to clear up a common misunderstanding. Your legs, feet, and skis do not have to be so close together they appear to be glued. The skis need only to be alongside and parallel to one another. They can be apart as much as 18 inches, and you can still make a good, solid parallel christie.

I agree it is pretty to watch a skier with his legs together. But for me, balance comes first, and when the *piste* gets rough I let my feet separate to the extent that I feel secure once again.

The key to parallel skiing is this: TURN BOTH YOUR FEET INTO THE TURNS AT THE SAME TIME. Make that task easier by *simultaneously unweighting both skis* and simultaneously changing the edges of both skis. I've explained all of these skills in earlier lessons.

Once you've started the christie properly, the remainder consists of nothing more than controlling the resulting side slip. And I've also explained that previously.

If you have trouble putting the skis together, by all means take a few lessons. You haven't mastered skiing until you have mastered the parallel christie.

TURNING IS WHAT SKIING IS ALL ABOUT

I must tell you that, since I hung up my racing skis, I have found a lot more pleasure in our sport. I also have to confess that I have learned a great deal about recreational skiing since I won those three gold medals. When I stop to think about it, I realize that I was lucky I could learn to ski without having to think too much about how to do it. I was able to give my entire concentration to the task of winning. Now, it is fun for me to watch people learning to ski, and I want to help them. Once, for example, I saw a man trying to teach his girl friend to ski on a hill that was just a bit too steep for her. She was scared and, of course, when one becomes scared, one loses confidence and learning becomes very difficult. This man would call to his friend, "turn, honey, turn." She wouldn't, and he became very provoked and told her how silly she was.

Well, turning is not that simple. Turning is what skiing is all about. Even today, when I go skiing, I work on my turns—christies, they are called. A christie is one of those pleasant-feeling turns in which you place your skis at a slight angle to your original direction to let yourself go into a skid. Then the trick is to control the skid. One of the ways to do that is with heel-push. In the illustration, you see me making a parallel christie to my left. My skis are resting slightly on their inside edges—the left ones in this case—and I am skidding, or sideslipping, around nicely. But suddenly I must make a much tighter turn to avoid an approaching obstacle. To do this, I heel-push. By comparing the two figures above, you can see how I have pushed my heels down the hill, pivoting them around the tips of my skis. To push the heels this way, I first bend my lower ankle away from the turn ever so slightly—my right ankle for this turn. (I've explained this procedure in more detail in an earlier lesson on sideslipping.) Then I lower my hips quickly by bending at the knees and, at the same time, I push the heels out from under me. But not too far! After all, I don't want snow in my back pocket! When I want the skis to stop skidding, I bend my ankle back inwards to make the inside edge of the ski grip the snow firmly. The upper ski also has to be able to skid, and I control its edge by moving my knee away from the turn. The movements are subtle. Practice is needed, and it's a good idea to have an instructor supervise your practice.

BANKING ROUND THE CONES

In some respects, skiing is like flying. When you fly a plane around a curve, you have to lean or bank it toward the inside of the turn. When you steer your skis into a curve, you have to "lean" them into the turn also. In the illustration you can see that for short radius turns, just the lower body leans in. For long radius turns, the whole body can lean in—or bank. This banking action does two things: First, it causes your skis to switch from one set of uphill (or inside) edges to the other set. (This procedure is called changing edges.) Second, it counteracts the forces which tend to throw you toward the outside of the turn. So, when you start to swing down a mountain, making long, fast parallel christies—tying together a whole series of turns—try to get the feeling that you are "banked" up against a large cone formed on the inside of your turn. It's a great sensation!

But be careful! If you lean to the inside too much, you'll fall to the inside. You can tell when you are banking too much because you'll feel more weight on your inside foot than on the outside. Remember—you should keep your weight evenly divided between each ski, or carry a bit more on the outside one.

SKIING ON HARD SNOW

Skiers dream of untracked powder snow. But let's face it, much of the time we're skiing on slopes that are hard and often icy and it's a real test of your equipment and technique. If in doubt, ask your ski instructor or someone in a ski shop to inspect your gear.

When your equipment is adequate, it is relatively easy to ski precisely on hard snow. To traverse, subtly increase the bite of your edges by using angulation. Push your knees into the hill while allowing your body to lean away from the

hill so that your shoulders become more or less parallel to the slope. Also keep your skis apart and weighted equally, with your weight pressing down over the whole of each foot, not just the toes or heels. This way you make the full bearing length of each edge bite the ice.

Turning on icy snow takes some special consideration, too. Look at the carved christie I am starting in the illustration. In the first figure, I'm in an angulated position with my hips forward (don't drop your derriere!) and skis apart and equally weighted. Next, I twist my feet and legs just enough to sort of sneak my skis into the fall line. I carefully avoid applying too much turning power to be sure that the skis will not skid out of my intended track. For the same reason, I use very little up-weighting. I do not want to turn my skis so much that they enter into an uncontrollable skid. Gentle precision is what I strive for, not brute haste. Once the turn is started, I rely on subtle forward pressure through the knees and ankles and the built-in turning action of the skis to complete the christie, just putting my skis in position to help them do their work. To do this, my hips must stay forward and my knees must move forward and toward the inside of the turn. This

re-angulation, as instructors call it, helps me concentrate most of my weight on the inside edges of my skis. If I find my skis tend to slip out from under me, then I press more on my lower ski, forcing its edge into the snow. If I still cannot hold and control my direction precisely, then I know that I have pushed the skis to their maximum potential, and I just have to learn to enjoy their limitation by sideslipping somewhat. But just to be sure, I always recheck my equipment if I'm not skiing the hard stuff as well as I think I should.

A KEY TO SKIING—UNWEIGHTING

Imagine a pair of ice skates with blades almost seven feet long. Imagine sleigh runners that same length. Now imagine trying to make those rigid runners or blades turn on snow.

Well, skis are almost that long, yet I can turn them in a flash. That's because they are flexible. Skis also have an arch (called a camber) built into them. The combination of the camber and the flexibility give the ski a certain amount of spring action. A good skier can use that spring—the rebound from his skis at the end of the turn—to make his skis come completely off the snow. This action is one of many forms of unweighting.

In the illustration, see how my skis are off the snow. At this moment, when my skis are unweighted, I can turn them quickly and easily in the direction I want to go. *Voila!*

Let me point out that it isn't necessary to take the skis off the snow when you want to make a parallel turn. I am doing it here because I must turn fast to hold my line through the slalom gates. Your instructor can show you how to make a quick upward or downward movement with your legs and body that will unweight your skis enough to turn them in most skiing situations. But, remember, for any kind of parallel turn work, you must use an unweighting action.

SQUARED TO YOUR SKIS

In this lesson I want to explain something about the terminology of skiing. Here, in the diagram, you see me just as I am finishing a parallel christie to my left, and at the very moment I am about to plant my pole for a christie to my right. Rather than speak of things as being "right" or "left"—which can become very confusing—we skiers like to use the words "inside" or "outside," the point of reference being the turn, or more precisely, the center of the turn. Thus, in the turn I have just finished, everything to my left (on the right, as you view things) is on the inside of the turn. (If I've already confused you, then reread what I have just said, to get the proper references straight in your mind.)

Note that my **inside** foot is ahead: so, of course, is my **inside** ski. But, also note that the difference is only a couple of inches. The board-like diagrams through my feet, knees, and shoulders, indicate how they too are ahead an equal amount, as they should be. Having everything on the inside ahead like this is called, being "squared to your skis," as opposed to being squared to your direction, which would put your body in line with the flat rectangular plane drawn about my figure.

I am just about to plant my **outside** pole which, once the new turn gets under way, will then be called my inside pole. As that turn progresses, everything which was on the **outside** will have to shift forward a few inches, since everything **inside** the turn should be ahead.

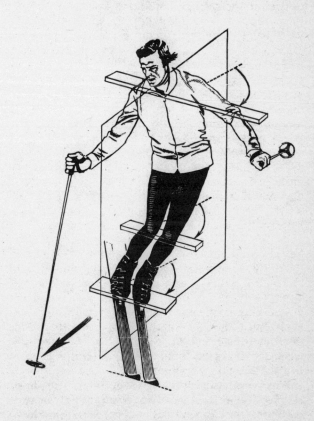

USE A WIDE STANCE FOR BALANCE

I would like to pass on to you a skiing tip that I learned from the coach of the French ski team, M. Honoré Bonnet. He advised me to ski with my feet apart. He said I was falling because I was losing my balance. And the reason I was losing my balance was that I was holding my feet together. And that, he said, interfered with the natural, independent working of the legs.

I had gotten into the feet-together habit, and it was hard to overcome. I was trying to race and look like a stylist. But once I really understood that, I didn't have any trouble in doing the right thing. Stand on your two feet, Jean-Claude, I said, and race.

I found the best stance for me was with my feet six to eight inches apart—seldom any closer than that, but often wider, as you can see from the illustration. Of course, if I want to ski in flashy style when skiing for pleasure, I can always glue my boots together, but I find that I lose freedom to change direction quickly and to maneuver in difficult passages. What's more, I really have to concentrate on keeping my balance.

Because of my experience, I suggest you learn to ski with your feet comfortably apart. When you feel at ease on the snow, then is the time to concentrate on looking stylish.

TURN, TURN, TURN!

I've said it before, but I'll say it again because it's so important: In skiing, the name of the game is turning. Sure, heading your skis straight down the fall line to go all out is a thrill. But you can't and won't want to do that all the time. Turn you must.

You may say that you turn because you have to avoid obstacles and want to follow a certain path or trail down the slope. This is true, certainly. But too few skiers realize that turning is the chief means of controlling your speed . . . you can go faster or slower merely by changing direction. If you want to slow down or stop, you turn toward the hill; or, as instructors say, turn off the fall line. If you want to gain speed, you head more down the hill or toward the fall line. And, when you want to maintain a constant speed, you must keep turning, alternately toward the hill, then toward the valley.

In the illustration, you see me turning with two purposes in mind: one, the intention of going fast, and the other of keeping a rein on my speed. The straight arrow marks the fall line (straight down) of this slope. In the left figure, I am about to turn toward the fall line (to my right). Since my intention is to ski rather fast, I won't turn much, and the curved arrow shows the course I will take. That's called skiing close to the fall line.

In the other figure my intention is to go slower, so I ski back and forth across the hill more, as you see by the dotted line showing again the course I will take. My turns now are more complete or rounded, and they take me farther away from the fall line (more into the hill) before I head back toward it. In this way I check my speed.

I believe many skiers hold back their progress by not thinking of how to use turns to control speed. Unfortunately, many beginning and intermediate skiers get into the habit of stemming for control, even when they are capable of doing parallel christies. If you are among this group, I hope you now see that you don't need the stem . . . you can get all the control you need by the amount you turn.

SCHUSS IT!

Speed! That's what skiing is all about. Wind in your face. Motion. You against the mountain. Unfortunately, the ski slopes of the world are becoming so crowded that going fast has become dangerous. The emphasis has had to shift to control—skiing in control. So the art of shooting (schuss, in German) straight down a ski slope has almost been lost. But don't you lose it. Anytime you find an opportunity to go straight down a slope without running into people, try it! Schuss it! But, build up your schussing skills and confidence gradually, first on short, easy slopes and gradually progressing to steeper and longer ones. Remember to keep your body centered between both skis at all times when schussing, with each foot almost directly under each hip. And keep your legs springy, extending them in the hollows of the terrain, as the illustration shows, but bending your knees adequately each time your ski tips reach a bump or mogul, to counteract the shock.

POLE-PLANT POWER

Sure, it is possible to ski without poles. In fact, often it's a good remedial exercise to do so, since it forces you to become more dependent upon good edge control. But you'll never become a good, polished skier, capable of handling all snow, all terrain, unless you learn to plant your pole correctly.

I like to think of my pole plant as a big, strong chain reaching from my shoulder, down through my arm, right to the snow via the ski pole. The feeling is one of tremendous power, of great control, coming through that arm. (By way of a reminder—it's always the inside pole that is planted. If you are about to turn right, then the right pole is planted; left turn, left pole.) Once you realize the role that the pole plant plays, perhaps you'll realize the importance of practicing to develop the right movements for pole-planting.

It's a timing device: the instant the pole stabs the snow is the moment when you must apply turning power to your skis.

It's an unweighting device: since you can apply a strong downward force to the planted pole, you can effectively help take much of your weight off the skis to make the task of turning them easier.

It's a shock-absorbing device: by varying the amount of pressure you apply to the pole, you can soak up with the muscles and joints of your arm some of the forces that develop when you set your edges.

It's a feeling device: just as you stab the snow, you can feel through that chain link the supporting quality of the snow. This tells you how much you have to unweight, or how much and how fast you must transfer weight from one ski to the other, or how far back or forward you can position yourself on your skis.

It's a banking device: it tells you how much to lean in toward the center of your turn.

It's a spotting device: in a manner of speaking, it spots the approximate center for your christies, giving you a place around which to turn.

And last, but not least, it's a device to help you regain balance.

CHECK SKI EDGES FOR MAXIMUM HARD-SURFACE HOLDING POWER

Sooner or later, all skiers encounter hard, sometimes icy, snow surfaces. So let me tell you how I am able to handle the hard stuff.

In the illustration, notice how my skis hold me into my turn. Part of the reason they do so is because I have always seen to it that my edges are not only kept sharp, but they are sharp in the right way. The cutaway drawings show how a good and a bad edge look. To provide maximum holding power, the bottom of the steel edges must be honed or filed so they are perfectly flush with the plastic surface of the ski sole. If the edge should protrude downward from the sole at any point, the protrusion would slow you down and give you trouble—*beaucoup de difficulté*—during your christies. Again, if the edge bottom has been filed so that it is less than flush with the sole, *mes amis,* you will have lost a great deal of holding power for any kind of snow. You will also lose holding power if the side of the edge is not filed to a right angle with the bottom, as shown in the cutaway of the bad edge.

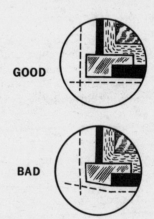

GOOD

BAD

I am neither a scientist nor an engineer, so I can only estimate, but I am quite convinced that if the edge is not flat to the bottom within a degree or two either way, your skis will not perform as well as they were designed to. If the angles are not correct, file them! If you don't know how, have either your instructor or your ski shop do the work for you.

As to the sharpness, that can be gauged by drawing your thumbnail across the edge. If it is sharp, it will shave off a thin white film from your nail. If it doesn't, don't expect to have your skis hold on the hard-packed surfaces. A sharpening job is in order.

You realize, of course, that I'm talking about deatils. But they are details where, as you Americans say, "the rubber meets the road." And if you'll forgive a breach of modesty, I didn't become a World Champion four times by ignoring details. For fun's sake, do yourself a favor. Check your edges now.

THE IMPORTANCE OF
EDGE CHANGING

It's one of the few unchanging rules of skiing that whenever you traverse a slope, your skis must rest on their uphill edges. This assures that you'll slide in the direction in which the skis point. When traversing with the up-slope to your left and the down-slope to your right, your skis must rest on their left edges. If you're traversing in the opposite direction, then your skis must rest on their right set of edges. Therefore, everytime you make a turn (a christie), linking a traverse in one direction with one in the other, somehow you must change the edges of the skis during the turn.

You do the same thing on ice skates when you turn from one direction to the other, but on ice skates the problem is simpler. After all, a skate blade is only one foot long, and skis are sometimes more than seven feet long. In a sense, a skier has seven times the edge control problem. Since a good skier turns much of the time—not only to avoid obstacles, but to control his speed—you can appreciate how important it is to master the changing of the edges.

In the illustration, you see me making a turn to my left. In the first figure, my skis are resting on their right edges. After my turn has been completed (last figure), they are resting on their left edges. Follow me through as I change

edges: Figure 1, I'm traversing the slope and I plant my ski pole to trigger a christie to my left. In Figure 2, the edge change has begun. Note how I've moved my body downhill—leaning into my turn slightly. I have also moved my knees toward the center of the turn. You can see how these movements have placed my skis flat to the slope. In the language of the ski instructor, I have banked my knees to release my edges. Once the skis are flat to the snow like this, I turn them easily. That puts me into the position you see in Figure 3. At this point, I have continued to bank with my body and my knees, and my skis now rest slightly on their *new* edges. The most difficult part of the turn is now over. From here on, I have only to control the skidding action and let the skis skid as much or as little as I want. In Figure 4, you can see almost all of the bottom of my skis because I have allowed the tails to skid around quite far so that I can traverse back across the ski slope without picking up too much speed.

There's more than one way to change edges—you can do it with one ski at a time. Then the turn is called a stem christie, not a parallel christie. With the latter, the action takes place in half the time. Therefore, you can get into your turns twice as fast. Now go to it!

AIDS FOR THE KICKTURN

A kickturn is a static turn; that is, you can't do one while under way. You must be standing still, sliding neither forward nor backward, to minimize the risk of toppling over as you alternately kick one ski then the other in the air and then fold it over to point in a direction opposite from which it started. Consequently, it pays to start from either a flat spot or from a position with both skis placed across the slope in a manner that will not allow them to slide forward, backward, or sideways. Next, the ski poles should be firmly planted, each on its own side. Then comes the kick, and it always surprises me how often even experienced skiers make it hard on themselves by not really kicking the ski—they merely try to pick it up and put it vertical to the slope before folding it over to its new position, parallel to, but pointing directly opposite to, the standing ski. In this lesson, you see me actually preparing to kick one ski up into the first position of this turn. Note that I swing my leg backward before I try to kick up the ski, very much as I would if getting ready to kick a ball. Beginners would do well to practice swinging each foot backward and forward a number of times—standing in a position similar to mine—to get the right feeling of having the ski swing freely to and fro without any wobbling of either the ski or the leg. Before long, the preparatory movement of swinging the leg backward will become a habit, saving lots of energy and effort for you.

WHEN THE GOING GETS ROUGH

Trouble can come in many forms—icy patches, unexpected changes in the steepness of the slope, bumps, ruts, and lots of other things. Your own mistakes can get you into trouble. Of course, the more alert you are, the more likely it is that you can avoid trouble. But don't bet on it. *Learn* to make a recovery.

The important thing is to stay cool. Almost always there's a little more time than you think there is. I know this because I have made lots of recoveries in slalom where there is supposed to be no time between turns. Many people have said to me, "Jean-Claude, those are wild recoveries you make," but I don't think they really understand. A recovery is a very unspectacular thing. Some of the turns that followed the recoveries may have been a little wild, but I was able to make them because I had already recovered. I was turning from a very solid stance.

Notice the illustration—it was made from a photograph showing me crossing some very bad ruts at high speed just before I was to make a turn to the right. I have dropped my hips very low—lowered my center of gravity—put my feet farther apart, and spread my arms a bit to make sure of my stability. I have pushed my left (uphill) ski ahead a bit so that a bump can't affect both legs simultaneously. And I also squared up my stance (I should have started to turn at this point) to make sure that I had completely recovered my balance. I was a fraction late in making the turn, but better a late turn than falling or making no turn at all.

You can learn to make recoveries like this, too. And since you don't have to make a gate as a racer does, you have even more time to recover before continuing your trip down the mountain.

THIS IS SLALOM

Gates are arranged into various combinations, the most frequent being the hairpin, the offset hairpin, the elbow, the flush, and the H-gate. The accompanying diagrams show how the poles for these various combinations would be set. The solid black dots indicate red flags; the open circles, blue gates.

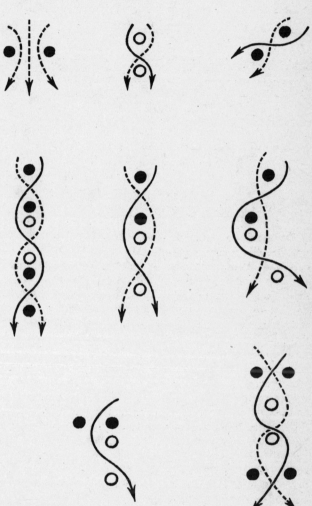

The first slalom race took place in Switzerland in 1922. It consisted of single poles placed here and there on a slope to force a skier to negotiate patches of rough snow or certain bumps or hollows. This form of competition was championed principally by the British, perhaps because one of their countrymen—Sir Arnold Lunn—was the man who first drew up the rules and finally refined and so promoted the event that it became part of the Olympic Winter Games of 1936. Ever since, the event has remained very much the same.

A modern slalom course consists of 55 to 65 slalom *gates*. Each gate consists of two 8- to 10-foot poles, with either red or blue flags attached, set vertically in the snow, 13 feet apart. The slalom racer must make both his feet and skis pass over the imaginary line between each pair of poles bearing flags of the same color. That is, the racer must go through each red gate and each blue gate. If a pole is straddled so that only one ski passes between the two poles, the competitor is disqualified.

There are basically three types of gates: open, closed, and oblique. Open gates are set at right angles to the fall line; closed gates are set in line with the fall line; and oblique gates may be positioned at any other angle to the fall line.

A world-class slalom event must be held on a fairly steep, almost icy slope with a vertical drop of 650 feet. Two courses are set, and each racer gets one run on each course, the winner being the person with the lowest cumulative time. Each course is usually negotiated by the top racers in close to one minute. A slalom racer's speed seldom exceeds 30 mph. You can see why a slalom racer must be very agile, since about one turn must be made every second.

DOWNHILL

In the world of ski racing, there are two different fields of competition—Alpine and Nordic. The Nordic events—cross country and jumping—have their roots in Norway. The Alpine events have theirs in the Alps of Europe. There are three Alpine races: slalom, giant slalom, and the downhill. I'd like to tell you about the premier event—the downhill.

Downhill competition somewhat like that of today began around the turn of the century in Austria and Switzerland. In those days, it used to take several hours to climb to the start of the courses—usually the top of the mountain. Everyone started at once, and the first one to reach the bottom some ten or 15 minutes later was the winner.

As competition became keener, that kind of a start proved dangerous, so the racers left the starting gate at one-minute intervals. Then equipment began to improve, so the racers went faster. So the courses had to be better prepared. And the rules clarified and formalized. Finally, downhill, combined with slalom, became an Olympic event in the winter of 1936 at Garmisch-Partenkirchen, Germany. That year, Birger Ruud, a Norwegian, won the downhill with a time of four minutes 47.4 seconds. But he did not win the combined medal, because he was too far back in slalom.

In 1948, the International Olympic Committee recognized the specialized nature of the two events and awarded medals for each one. When I won a gold medal for this event at the Olympic Winter Games in 1968 at Grenoble, France, my time was 1:59.85. It is not fair to compare times from one course to the other, or even on the same course from year to year, because too many things change and dangerous corners are eliminated, snow conditions are never the same, trees are cut out to make certain passages safer, and so the courses have been shortened. I mention the times to point out how much faster today's downhillers go. Now, it's not uncommon for a racer to be clocked at more than 80 mph! And on several of the world's great courses, the *average* speed of the fastest finishers is 60 mph, or better.

Through the years, many competitors have been killed on downhill courses—not surprising when you realize how fast they go. Next time you go motoring along at 70 mph, try to imagine what that would be like on just two narrow skis—not on the highway, but on a steep, bumpy course. Is it any wonder downhillers must wear crash helmets? Or why the downhill is considered the premier Alpine event?

GIANT SLALOM

The giant slalom, or GS, as American and Canadian racers call this event, is a late addition to Olympic skiing competitions. Both the downhill and the slalom first became a part of those once-every-four-years Winter Games back in 1936. But the GS wasn't added until 1952 at Oslo, Norway.

The giant slalom, as its name implies, is something more than slalom, and it's something less than downhill. A typical international class GS course will consist of 45 gates set on a mountain with a minimum vertical drop from top to bottom of 1350 feet. A downhill must drop 3500 feet and only a handful of control gates are used. Those figures compare with the minimum international-class requirements for a slalom of 600 feet of vertical drop with 60 to 70 gates.

You can tell immediately that since the GS has far fewer turns to negotiate, and since no tricky combinations of gates are permitted, the turns must be longer and the speed about twice as fast as in the slalom. In GS, the average speed is about 40 mph. Most courses are negotiated in about one minute and a half. In recent years there has been a marked trend to make the courses somewhat shorter and give each racer two runs—with the fastest total time determining the winner.

The GS is not a downhill, though on steep sections of a course racers occasionally endure short speed bursts through the gates—which are set a minimum of 15 feet apart—at close to 60 mph. Since the turns are sharper than for a downhill, it takes a technically proficient, strong, and courageous skier to win a gold medal in GS—someone with reflexes perhaps not quite as fast as those of a slalom skier, and with the ability to withstand the stresses of speed almost as well as a downhiller.

I won an Olympic gold medal in each of the three Alpine events, not because I was a natural at all three (slalom was the most natural for me) but because I studied carefully the special needs of each event and for years trained hard and carefully for each one of them. Maybe you could do the same—if you wanted to.

THE ROLE OF THE INSIDE SKI

Whenever you traverse across a slope, the upper ski must always be ahead, but by no more than half a boot-length. That applies, no matter what direction you traverse. The relative position of the skis allows you to stand solidly, with both knees and ankles equally bent. When the mountain is to your right, then the upper ski is the right one and it must lead. When the mountain is to your left, then it's the left ski which is the leading upper ski. That means that when you make a downhill turn, what was once the leading uphill ski gradually becomes the following lower ski. And, or course, what was once the following downhill ski becomes the inside ski of the turn and it must move ahead of the other to become the leading ski as soon as the new traversing direction is established.

But when does it go ahead? Actually, in a perfectly executed parallel christie, it should gradually and automatically creep ahead as the turn progresses. This is so since both skis are traveling at the same speed and both skis are given the same turning impetus: the inside ski having less distance to travel around the curve, will then gradually creep ahead.

Aside from these natural dynamics of the turn, there is a practical advantage to always having one ski slightly ahead of the other. That is, with the upturn at the tips of the skis, they are less likely to cross over one another. In fact, when skiing on some very lively skis, especially metal ones, I find it a distinct help to artificially move ahead my inside ski before I am facing the fall line. But mind you, it should only be a matter of an inch or two, and it must be done very quickly, just as the skis start into the new turn. Some of you, too, might find this tip useful.

BETTER BALANCE FOR BETTER SKIING

No doubt you've heard it said, if you can walk you can ski. It's true, especially today, because now not only do ski boots give even the weakest of ankles more support than they need, but three, four, or five-foot skis make controlling speed and stopping easy for almost everyone. But skiing well is a question of degree, and as most skiers know, the better you ski, the more fun you have.

A major key to unlocking the mysteries of better skiing is balance, and balance, contrary to popular belief, can be improved by improving your skills. But you must work at it with special exercises. Here's a simple one that has helped thousands of skiers raise their level of pleasure. It's an exercise that violates one of the cardinal rules of our sport: Namely, that one always keep more weight on the downhill ski.

That rule is well and good, but what happens if you can't keep more weight on the downhill ski? Sure, you're likely to fall unless you practice balancing on the uphill edge of your uphill ski. Then, at least, you won't be caught by surprise and you should be able to regain your balance quickly. Here's what to practice: First, choose a smooth-packed, intermediate slope, preferably a short one served by uphill transportation. Then leave your ski poles with the lift attendant and go up. On the way down, make a series of medium-speed traverses while deliberately picking up your lower ski, as I demonstrate here. There are two things to note and imitate carefully: 1) The upper ski is carefully positioned on its uphill edge with your weight firmly distributed over the entire sole of your foot; 2) The upper body has to be positioned so that your center of gravity rests directly over the standing foot. Practice this exercise to both the left and the right, without poles and with poles, and soon you'll never be caught by surprise when you inadvertently get more weight on the uphill ski. And when you are not surprised, it's very easy to recover from a temporary loss of balance. And "no-fall" skiing is more fun and much safer.

BE SURE YOUR BINDINGS WORK; YOUR SAFETY IS AT STAKE

These days, there is no excuse for anyone to ski without using reliable release bindings; there are so many good ones available. Some people call these safety bindings, but they are not necessarily safe. If they are not adjusted properly, they can release inadvertently—when you don't expect it—and you can be hurt. Very early in my racing career, I learned to check my bindings very closely and regularly. I had had the misfortune not to be able to finish races because my bindings released when they shouldn't have. Tremendous twisting forces are involved in making a fast, precise slalom turn. In the illustration, you can see how my whole body is beginning to twist to my left, while my skis are still turning to my right. If my bindings weren't adjusted properly, I could twist out of them, fall and, at the very least, lose the race!

Train yourself to check your bindings regularly—ideally, every time you put on your skis. Otherwise, at least check them before each day of skiing. Check for equal right and left release. If the toe unit of your binding is mounted crooked by as little as 1/16 of an inch, or if the notches on your boot are not equal, the bindings will not release equally to the left and to the right. You'll come out too early on one side and, thinking they're set too loose, you'll tighten up on the adjustment screw. This may make release to the other side impossible. You're in for trouble! And coming out of a binding when you don't want to can be almost as dangerous. In fact, do yourself a favor—have your bindings checked by a simple machine which is carried by most shops which seriously specialize in skiing equipment.

3-The Advanced Skier

SHAPE UP FOR SKIING

Skiing today is much easier than it used to be, because the equipment is so much better. The new plastic boots give even a beginner almost more control than is needed for the first year or so of skiing. And the new short skis are much easier to turn than the seven-foot monsters which I and many of my contemporaries had to use for racing not so many years ago. All in all, now you don't have to be an athlete to learn to ski. Today, you can have lots of fun with less work.

Now that doesn't mean that you can go on forever having skiing fun without doing something to keep in shape. It's not that skiing is all that difficult. It's that if you are in sound physical condition you can do more things and have even more pleasure. It's also true that when in shape you are much less likely to get hurt when you take a tumble.

Being in shape doesn't necessarily mean that you are strong. Of course, any good physical fitness program will include exercises such as weight lifting to help you build up specific muscles needed for a sport, as well as the necessary support muscles—and for skiing, that's most of the body's muscles.

A good program must also include plenty of exercises to stretch your muscles. It is true that too much incorrect weight lifting, for example not following a contraction exercise with an extension exercise, does make you sort of muscle-bound so that the muscles won't stretch out as much as they should—meaning that you could hurt or tear even your strongest muscles if they haven't been properly conditioned.

And, finally, a good conditioning program will help you develop endurance, so that you can keep up your sports activities long enough to enjoy them without injury to your heart. One of the best forms of conditioning for this is jogging.

If you plan to ski often this season, I urge you to make an extra effort to stay in shape. There are lots of fine books in the library to help you develop your own program. Why not start one, today?

SUPPORT FROM YOUR POLE

Everytime I make a turn, I use my ski poles to good advantage. So should you. When I turn to the left, I jab my left pole in the snow. When I turn to the right, it's the right pole that gets jabbed.

I jab it for several reasons: For one, to act as an indicator for my turn as a jab serves as a sort of pivot point around which my skis will describe an arc. For another, as a timing device, I know that the instant my pole jabs in, it's time to start my skis turning in the new direction. And finally, I take support on the pole to help me unweight the skis so they'll turn more easily, and to help me modify my body position in preparation for the next turn.

It's important to know where to plant the pole, and that place varies with your speed and in relation to your position with the fall line. In general, the faster you go, the further forward it can be planted and the slower you go, the further back it can be planted. In no event, however, do you ever plant it further forward than about one foot behind the tips of the skis, or further back than about opposite the middle of the feet. You must always plant the pole on the downhill side of your skis—about one foot away when skiing close to the fall line, and about three feet when very far off it (as when approaching your next turn from almost a straight position across the slope).

And as a final word of caution: never let your pole planting arm get further back than the corresponding shoulder. To do so is to risk loss of control.

WHERE TO PLANT YOUR POLE

When a skier starts to perfect the christies . . . those graceful, sweeping, skidding turns . . . it's time to learn to use a ski pole as sort of an axis. Jab a pole into the snow . . . the one closest to the center of the turn . . . then turn around it. The planted pole serves as a sort of axle, your arm acts like the spoke of a wheel and you and your skis are out on the rim. In this lesson I'm going to show you something about where the pole should be planted in relation to your body and your skis.

Actually, part of how and where you plant your pole is personal preference, and I can't tell you to do it exactly like me. However, I think the illustrations show a general rule that applies to everyone. The rule is: plant your pole at such a point that a line joining it to about the center of your skis would constitute the fall line. The illustration explains it better. Notice the line running down the hill from where my feet are. That's the fall line going directly down the hill which I've described in earlier lessons. I've planted my pole on this imaginary line approximately an arm's length away from my feet. (The top one of the three diagrams

shows my position for the christie I'm doing in the full illustration.) The line running through my foot, at the center of the ski, is the fall line and the circle is where I plant my pole. In the second diagram, the skis are pointing more across the hill as I prepare to plant my pole, so following the rule, the pole is planted right down the fall line from my foot. The third diagram shows where I would plant my pole if I were heading straight across the hill at the start of the turn. Simple, isn't it?

The way you plant your poles can vary, according to your needs. For example, you can use the planting as an aid to the upward movement in up-unweighting. Or, to get acceleration in doing a racing turn, Or, you can place the pole off more to the side to assist with a quick change of edge. Skillful pole planting, of course, takes practice, but it also take strength in your arms, shoulders, and chest. To improve, you may need special strengthening exercises such as push-ups. Whether you need exercise and what sort you need, I can't advise in a broad-scoped book directed at all skiers. It's best to take the advice of someone who knows his skiing and ski teaching, and who has seen you ski.

POLE PLANT—
A KEY TO PRECISION SKIING

If you plan to ski fast and on the steep slopes—and who doesn't?—you must master pole planting.

To make your poles work for you, they have to be the right length. They should pass comfortably under your armpit when you are standing upright. They can even be an inch or two shorter. If they are too long, they will throw you on your *derrière*.

Think of pole planting as a commitment to turn. You spot the place you want to turn. You prepare and, when you reach the spot, the pole closest to the center of your turn is planted hard. *Pow!* You unweight, change edges, and are off in a new direction almost before you know it . . . if you do it right.

Fall line

Make it a habit from the very beginning to use your whole arm to make the pole reach the spot. Don't reach with only the tip of the pole by bending your wrists this way and that. It will rob your pole plant of much of its effectiveness if your hand is out of line with your forearm.

In the illustration, you can see just how effective pole plant can be. I am on a steep slope. On the left, I have firmly gripped the snow with my edges and just planted the pole. In the middle drawing, the pole plant is beginning to take effect. I begin to raise my knees to unweight (you can see this by looking at my legs). I absorb part of the energy of the pole plant with my shoulders and I rotate them in the direction of the turn. In the illustration on the right, I am bracing hard against the pole and my skis come off the snow. It is now easy to change edges and complete my turn.

Pole planting is not hard to do, but difficult to perfect. But perfect it you must if you want to ski like a professional.

BUILDING SKILLS FOR SKIING

What's true for so many things is also true for skiing—the better you get, the more enjoyable it becomes. I often wonder why so many people seem to forget that. All day long they slide down the same slopes doing the same old things. I have to agree, it is fun to feel the wind in your face and just ski down, doing as little as possible. But I think that the people who do this do so because they lack the confidence to do otherwise. And they lack confidence because they lack skills. Yet skills are things which can and should be practiced—by everybody.

Two of the most important skills of skiing are edge control and balance. Both will improve with practice, making you not only a better skier, but one who gets more pleasure from our sport. And one of the best exercises I know to help you build these skills simultaneously is to practice skiing on one ski, particularly on your uphill ski. Proceed as follows:

Choose a well-packed, smooth, gentle slope. Ski across the slope as you normally would, but every so often pick up the lower ski, learning to balance while riding on only the upper edge of the upper ski. Practice this while traversing both to the left and the right.

Next, practice skating into the hill. Traverse, as above, then push off your lower ski into a small skating step. You may find your balance improves if you twist your upper body slightly toward the direction in which you push off, just as for ice skating.

Next, gradually steepen the angle of traversing till eventually you can skate into the hill from heading straight down the fall line. (At first, you may find these exercises easier to do without poles.)

Finally, traverse the slope, skate into the hill, then swing back your lower ski.

You'll find that after practice of this sort you'll be able to recover very quickly from a mistake, whereas once you would have fallen. You'll not only ski better, you'll enjoy it more.

SECRETS FOR EASY PARALLEL

In this lesson, you see me from a three-quarter overhead view. I have just started to turn into an easy downhill parallel christie. I use the word "easy" advisedly because this turn is easily accomplished—once you develop the necessary skills for it. Those are: the ability to move your weight forward or backward on your skis, as needed; the ability to sideslip in a curve; the ability to plant your ski pole; and finally, the ability to turn both your skis at the same time while keeping them more or less parallel.

The first secret to making parallel christies easy for yourself is to start the turn on the correct spot. That spot is never in a hollow or trough. It is *always* on a nice, small, friendly bump or knoll. You see, if your timing is correct, you can use the crest of the bump as a pivot point around which to swivel both ends of the skis.

And what is the correct timing? It's this: you must start the skis turning the very instant that you feel the crest of

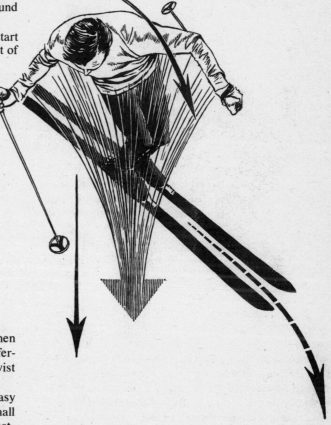

the bump directly underfoot. This is the moment when the fronts and tails of your skis will be off the snow, offering no resistance to lateral displacement. You simply twist your legs and feet around at this moment.

There is another secret to be learned for this kind of easy parallel and it's called "anticipation." Because most small bumps offer only momentary support, you must act fast. You have barely one-tenth of a second to get the turn started. That means your pole must already be planted, right on the crest, a foot or two below your feet. Also, your entire upper body must be anticipating the turn by twisting and leaning toward the direction you want to go, as you see me doing in the accompanying illustration.

Once you get the turn started, of course, all you then have to do is let the skis sideslip as much or as little as you want. The thing that makes this turn so easy to start is that by using the bump as an underfoot pivot, you do away with any need to bounce up or down to unweight the skis.

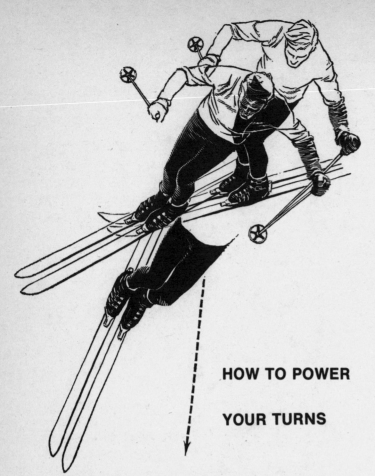

HOW TO POWER

YOUR TURNS

ANOTHER KEY TO SKIING— EDGE CHANGE

When you ski straight down a slope, you are schussing. When you ski across a slope, you are traversing. When you traverse, with the hill to your left, your skis correctly rest on their left, or uphill edges. In France, we call those edges *les carres amont*. When you make a turn and traverse in the opposite direction, so that the hill is now to your right, the skis must rest on the other set of edges—again, those on the uphill side. But remember, the uphill side is now to your right.

During the turn, a *changement des carres*—a changing of the edges—has taken place. In the illustrations, I show how I change edges by using a banking action. Just like a boy on a bicycle, I lean my body into the turn. The leaning action causes my skis to roll from one set of edges to the other set. Here, you see me during the half-second which it takes to change the edges during a normal parallel christie, my skis rest on their uphill edges. By visualizing how my body has moved from that position into the second, you will see the banking action. I actually lean sideways—away from the hill and down toward the valley—just enough to make the skis roll from their uphill edges, flatten on the snow, and then on over to the new set of edges. My ski pole gives me a moment's support and prevents me from banking too much. Remember, you must change edges for every christie you make.

A christie is a smooth, sliding or carving turn, usually performed with the skis held more or less parallel throughout. To start your skis into one, there are three basic things to do. First, lighten the load resting on the skis by unweighting. Second, and at the same time, partially roll the skis over to their other set of edges. (I've discussed both these basics in earlier lessons.) And while in the midst of these two processes, apply turning power to your skis to start them skidding or carving around.

There are several ways to achieve this turning power. A popular method is to quickly shift your weight to the outside or "turning" ski. This is what is often done for the snowplow and the stem turns. Still another way is to push one foot laterally to the outside of the turn, using the front of the ski as a movable pivot. This is called stemming. A variation of this is to thrust aside the heels of both skis. That's logically called heel pushing. It is also possible to swivel both ends of the skis around their middles merely by twisting or rotating the feet and knees in the desired direction. And, though it complicates the understanding of turning power and its sources, it's also possible to use your arms, shoulders and torso as a source of rotary power.

My preference is using a combination of movements. First, as I bring one christie to a definite set of edges, I lightly twist my upper body in the direction in which I intend to turn. Instructors call this anticipation. Then, during the brief period that my skis have been unweighted, I twist or crank my knees and feet around in the direction which my upper body has already begun to move. In this way, my upper body never gets behind my feet, and maintaining balance and control over the skis becomes an easy matter.

CONTROLLING YOUR CHRISTIES

One of the necessary skills worth developing involves the ability to shift weight from one ski to the other. The better the skier you are, the more subtly you will do this procedure. Of course, every time you make a christie, one of those swooshing turns, your weight has to be shifted from what at the start of the turn was the downhill ski to the other one which, as your turn progresses, becomes the new downhill ski. (That ski is referred to as the outside ski of the turn.) The amount that you can control the radius of your turn depends on how much and how fast you transfer weight to that outside ski.

In the illustration you see me carving a turn to my right. I have just crossed over the imaginary fall line which runs directly down the slope. Note the bend of my outside ski. It has a much deeper curve to it than the inside ski. That's because I've put more weight on it by pressing down more with my left or outside leg than with the right one. By varying this pressure, I can cause the outside ski to bend more or less. The more it bends the sharper becomes the radius of my turn and the slower I go. The less I exert pressure, the shallower the turn becomes and the faster I go. So you see, with this subtle shifting of weight I can not only vary my path to avoid obstacles or just enjoy the thrills of turning, but I can control my speed as well. Weight shifting is certainly a worthwhile skill to develop, wouldn't you say?

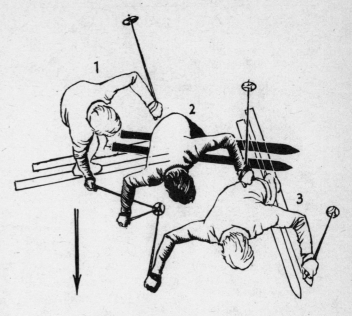

AN INSTANT TURN FOR MOGUL SKIING

A mogul is a skier-made bump. A mogul is usually never found in the singular; moguls come in groups and usually are the biggest and most numerous on the steepest of slopes. They get there from the cutting, gouging, and pushing action exerted by the passage of hundreds of skis. First, the skis cut ruts, and the snow from the ruts gets pushed into heaps. As the heaps get packed down, more skiers turn on them and as their skis come around the heaps, they drop into the ruts. The ruts become grooves, and the snow pushed there gets packed onto the existing heaps. On steep slopes, the skis exert more carving action so the moguls get bigger and bigger and the grooves get deeper and deeper.

There is only one safe and easy way to ski these fields of moguls, and that's by turning both skis at the same time—that is, parallel. The skis don't have to be close together, mind you, but you must turn them both simultaneously and fast, for if you don't turn right now (when your feet are on the crests of the moguls) your feet will not get your skis around fast enough to follow the next groove. Failure to do that almost always results in a fall.

How do you start into your turns fast? The illustration—an overhead view—shows how to do it. My ski pole, the inside one of the turn, is planted on the crest of the mogul, and immediately I start to "anticipate" the new direction with my upper body. Can you see how I have moved my head, arms and chest downhill? I do so with a combination banking and twisting motion. A moment later, when my feet also get to the crest of the mogul, the anticipation causes both ends of the skis to swivel around directly under foot, and *voila!* I'm into my new turn in plenty of time to follow the groove.

A MODERN TURN

The christie you see me performing here is not only fun—it's almost a necessity for all good skiers. In French it's called an *avalement* christie (say A-Val-mon, pronouncing the first two A's as in valley) because the word means swallowing. The turn is used for "swallowing" those big skier-made mounds—moguls—which build up so quickly on today's steep ski slopes. The swallowing is done by the legs, of course, with the knees bending deeply to act as shock absorbers. The shock-absorbing action allows you at all times to keep your skis in contact with the snow, which means that you can ski with the maximum of control.

Before you can master this exciting, useful christie, you first need to know how to make a basic parallel christie. Then you need to know how to down-unweight, and how to anticipate. Down-unweighting, as the words imply, is a means of momentarily taking your weight off your skis by a very quick downward movement. In the illustration, note how I am standing rather tall as I ski through the hollow immediately preceding the swelling of the mogul. By the time my skis are on the crest of the hump, you can see that my hips are lower than my knees. It's this apparent down motion of the hips which simultaneously unweights the skis and absorbs the shock of running up the bump. Actually, what usually happens is that you allow the bump to quickly force up your skis, feet, and knees while your hips remain at about the same level.

While these movements are taking place, you must also anticipate—that is, twist your upper body in the desired direction, so that at the instant your skis are unweighted (at the crest of the mogul) they will swivel into the turn. Then, as your skis skid or carve around the steep back side of the mogul, you once again gradually extend the legs—and get set to "swallow" the next mogul.

WORK SKIS FOR BEST PERFORMANCE

I want to come directly to the point—there is no single turn or technique which can be used for every situation in skiing. Thank goodness for that! Otherwise skiing would become *trés ennuyeux*—very boring. For me, the fascination of skiing is the thrill of speed, the excitement of competition, and the sense of being master of the mountains. But it's only possible to taste these joys completely once you have learned to work your skis for each of the constantly changing situations.

In the illustration, see how I have raised my right knee and foot so that only a slight amount of weight rests on the front part of the right ski. That ski—the one on the inside of my christie—held momentarily in the position shown, acts as a stabilizer for my balance. Here, I am putting the outside ski—my left one in this instance—to work. By placing most of my weight on that ski, I cause it to bend deeply and I force its edge to bite the snow firmly. As a consequence, my skis and I turn more sharply. If I start to turn too sharply, I need only to press my inside ski back to the snow to equalize my weight over each ski. Then neither ski will bend as much as the outside one did before, and I'll make a longer turn. Shifting weight back and forth between the skis can be done less obviously than I can demonstrate in this lesson. Each situation is different. You must learn to feel how your skis respond to your shifts of weight and work them accordingly.

YOU AND THE MOGULS AND THE FALL LINE

Skiing the moguls, when you know how to, is one of the most exciting things about our sport. It is not easy for many skiers, however, because they never learned how to turn both skis at the same time—never learned how to make parallel christies, in other words. You must know how to do this because that's the only way it is possible to turn fast enough to keep your skis on the snow and follow down through the snake-like troughs between moguls. Otherwise, the moguls act like small ski jumps and launch your skis into the air—which soon leads to trouble.

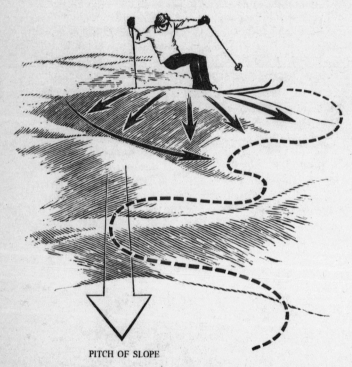

PITCH OF SLOPE

In an earlier lesson, I explained about the fall line—it's an imaginary line of the slope, or the path a free-rolling ball would take from wherever you are standing. On a smooth slope, the fall line goes straight down the slope, but in the illustration you can see from the arrows that the fall line goes in many different directions. Since every time your skis turn into and off the fall line you must switch them from the edges on one side to those on the other, you can now perhaps begin to understand why it's so easy to get into trouble when mogul skiing—unless you know how to turn your feet and skis quickly. I'd like to urge you to take lessons and learn to do that, because mogul skiing certainly is wonderfully rewarding.

MORE ON MOGUL SKIING

I've written about mogul skiing in previous lessons and have said that unfortunately there is no easy way to learn to ski them. Besides, if the moguls are big and plentiful, you have to be a better than average skier before you can even begin to tackle them, let alone enjoy them. As a starting point, you should know how to make consistent parallel christies.

A glance at the illustration should reveal to you that you must be strong and athletic enough to move your body quickly into what, at first, will feel like awkward positions. Part of the reason for this is that the skis must rise up and over the bumps without much disturbance to the mass of weight contained in the torso, head and arms. Otherwise, you're apt to lose balance. In effect, the legs must act as shock absorbers, soaking up any potential unbalancing jolts. What you have to do is to compress the body on the crests of the moguls (like doing deep knee bends), and extend the legs as the skis travel through the hollows or troughs between the humps.

A word of caution—don't try to ski with your feet and legs too close together. It's very possible that because of the way the mogul appears to change its shape rapidly as you carve around it, that your ski tips might be forced into crossing one another. That's nothing serious if you are aware of what's happened, and can move quickly enough to uncross them. But if you're not able to quickly untangle them you'll probably have to shake the snow out of your ears shortly after.

Another point—keep your eyes down-slope, seeking out your path well in advance of the time you get there, looking for the most favorable places to make your turn. And remember, the easiest place and time to turn the skis is at the instant your feet reach the crests of the humps.

THE FLAT SKI MYTH

Have you ever heard the expression, "ski on a flat ski?" It's quite a popular notion, even among some people who are experts about ski techniques. According to these people, I won three Olympic gold medals because I rode a flatter ski than anyone else. Well, if that's how I won, it's news to me unless I don't understand the phrase "flat ski."

Just look at the illustration: I'm cutting hard and fast through a gate during one of the man-to-man professional slalom races. Do my skis seem flat to the snow? Of course they don't. The edges (the inside-of-the-turn edges) are holding fast, and my skis are tilted over almost 45 degrees. They have to be. They have to resist the tremendous centrifugal force that builds up in a turn. This force can push you to the outside of the turn and into a skid. And as every skier knows, when you and your skis skid, you lose time and sometimes control. Consequently, a racer must carve a turn, making the edges of the skis bite into the snow and ice. So how can the skis be flat?

Granted, if you edge your skis too much you'll eventually tip them over enough to ride on their sides, and that would slow you down. In fact, it would knock you off balance because your skis would slip out from under you. However, I see far more racers and recreational types who skip around in their turns with skis edged too flat, rather than over-edged.

As far as I'm concerned, there are only two moments when your skis should be flat or not edged: when you are schussing down the fall line, or during that very brief instant when you start into a turn and roll the skis from one set of edges to the other. So just remember, you have to edge your skis to carve your christies.

SKI TALL, SKI SMALL AND ADAPT TO TERRAIN

Sometimes I ski standing tall. At other times I crouch low. I don't do this just because of some whim. My position varies because the terrain varies.

Here you see me demonstrating the extremes of both positions. If you want to become an expert skier, you will have to make use of these extremes in the way you stand on your skis. If the terrain is smooth, stand tall and let the springiness which the knees and ankles provide go to work for you, absorbing the minor bumps and hollows which are always present. If the terrain is rough, let your legs buckle-up deeply underneath you whenever you feel that the bumps want to compress you. You would be surprised how many good skiers won't let their bodies fold up as much as I let mine. There are times that they should.

Your body must never become frozen into a tall or a small position. It must vary—*toujours*—all the time, flexing up and down so that your skis, and your head, get as smooth a ride as possible. That way, you'll ski better, faster, and safer.

Because I have skied for fun and in competition since I was 3 years old, skiing is second nature to me. I no longer think about the position of my arms, legs, and body. What I do think about when I race is the course ahead of me, and I had to train myself to concentrate on that. And I think it is important for all skiers, from beginners to Olympic champions.

SKIING THE SUPER STEEP

During the last few years or so a few very fine skiers have sought to prove that "nothing is impossible until it is proved impossible." These skiers chose to test themselves and their doctrine on some of the steepest slopes of the European Alps, on Alaska's Mount McKinley, and Washington State's Mount Rainier. One moment of poor judgment, bad timing, or physical weakness on some of these precipitous places could mean the end of a skier's life.

Of course, not everyone wants to risk everything to prove that the world's steepest slopes can be skied. Sometimes, it seems enough just to be able to get down the steeper sections of those trails and slopes marked as "expert" by the ski areas. That is, until you develop a few basic special skillls, acquire some knowledge about what to do, and then practice on progressively steeper pitches, building up your confidence as you go.

The basic techniques are really nothing new to any skier. But you must train yourself to ski more slowly, and with more traversing between turns. In the illustration, any skier should recognize two of the standard basics: My feet and legs are apart, and I have about two-thirds of my weight on the lower ski. When it's steep, you can't risk getting the boots or skis entangled with each other just because you want to look good, nor can you risk having your skis slip out from under you because you lean uphill and put too much weight on the uphill ski. The risk is not in the fall itself but in the fact that once down, you might quickly slide out of control and hit something.

Look at the illustration again. Not every skier will note how I hold my uphill pole, but it's almost parallel to the slope, so that I can quickly swing it around at the right time without its catching in the snow. If it did catch, the delay could force a fall or cause me to turn much less than I need to in order to keep my speed within safe limits. Now look at that downhill pole. It's planted very firmly because I might have to actually jump the skis off the snow and use that pole as a vertical axle around which to swing body and skis into the next traverse. By doing that I (and you) can ski down even the super steeps while keeping your speed about two mph.

In this illustration, I am about to go into a turn. But see where I am looking—not where I am, but where I will be. I have trained myself to look at least two turns ahead. So should you, and I would like to tell you why.

If you look only where you are—at your feet or your ski tips—when making a turn, you will not know exactly how much to turn and you won't be able to anticipate bumps, ruts, ice, and changes in pitch. And if you don't know these things are coming up, you will not be able to ski smoothly and rhythmically.

You must train yourself to look where you will be so that, like a racer, you can plan your "line." As soon as you spot a good place to turn, ski toward it, but immediately start looking for the next place to turn so that you know how much turn you need to get there. Look ahead and you will be able to determine this.

TO WIN—CONCENTRATE

I am often asked how I was able to come out top man on the professional ski racing circuit, winning more than $68,000 after not racing for more than four years? To be brief—I did it the same way I won three Olympic gold medals at the Grenoble Winter Games in 1968: I did it by concentrating.

To win, for me at least, requires concentration on every detail. Before the season starts, I concentrate on making my skiing muscles very strong and my endurance better than anyone else's. Early in the winter, I concentrate on getting together not just the best equipment, but the best equipment for me. The only way I know of to do that is to try out as many pairs of skis as I can. And of course, I must have boots that allow me to ski precisely and that don't hurt my feet too much. Anyone who wants to win, I believe, can do no less.

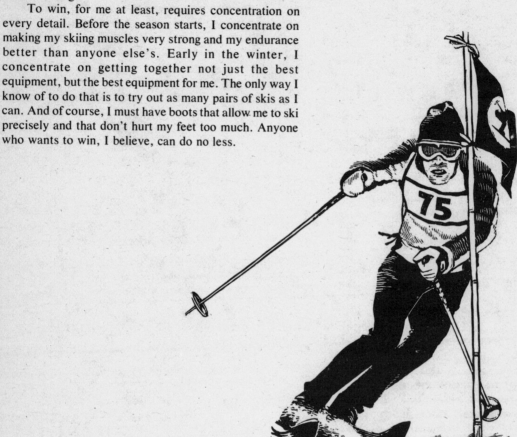

Then come techniques—the things one does to get to the bottom faster than anyone else. Every move made on a race course must be carefully planned beforehand. Study each course. Concentrate on discovering the fastest line through the course, and then memorize it. You should do this in such a way that years later you'll remember almost every detail.

One of my secrets for winning is this: Once on the course, I concentrate on getting the skis closer to the gates than anyone else. You must train yourself to compare yours with those of anyone who beats you. Once you *know* that you can cut your skis closer to the slalom poles than the other competitors, you'll have such confidence that you'll be able to concentrate on other details, such as getting a winning start and planning your finish-line strategy—things I'll tell about in other pointers.

IT TAKES A QUICK START TO WIN

I have a small confession to make—I believe I won many races not necessarily because I was a faster skier than some of the world's best, but because I concentrated on every single detail, and did something to improve upon each one of them.

Take starts, for example. Sometimes the wand that goes across your knees and trips the start switch when you move out did not stretch all the way across both legs. In those instances, I learned how to swing out first the leg that was free of the wand. In this way I believe I gained several hundredths of a second. There was no rule against doing this. Anyone could have done it, if they had only concentrated on such details. It wasn't long before others spotted my advantage and so wands were built to stretch all the way across the start gate.

Fine. I invented a new start, like the one you see me doing in the illustration. I placed my poles in the snow ahead of the wand—perfectly legal—and on "GO" I leap up into the air, taking support on my poles. Then, when my boots trip the electric timing wand, I am about two feet higher than I'd be otherwise. That extra height, I'm sure, translates into a faster get-away speed, and gives me almost a half-second advantage over my competitors. But remember, first it takes a lot of concentration on the details, and then it takes a lot of practice to perfect them. You must figure out where *you* should plant *your* poles, how hard and how high to jump, and how much forward lean to use. But it's not impossible. Go out and practice, trying each time to improve on just one small part at a time. Soon, you too will learn to get out of the start faster than a scared rabbit.

TO WIN—FINISH FAST

In almost every slalom or giant slalom race the longest distance between any two sets of gates is that between the finish line and the last gate. It's often as much as 30 yards, a distance that takes about two or three seconds to cover at slalom speeds. You win or lose a race in much less time than that, so it's well worth it to plan your finish line strategy very carefully.

Sometimes the best thing to do is to cut the last gate as close as you can, and proceed to the finish in a straight line—but do so in a tuck position to cut down on wind resistance.

Other times, especially when the distance is almost flat, as it usually is, you may want to skate to the finish line. I usually do, as you see me doing here. But notice how I keep my body very low to streamline myself. I would do better to keep my ski poles more streamlined too, although at slalom speeds (25 to 30 mph) the wind resistance on them is not too great.

But I must warn you about skating: Unless you have very powerful and fast legs you can easily slow yourself down. After all, your skis must travel a longer distance when skating than when going straight. So learn your limits—learn to feel at what speeds you can accelerate when skating and at what point you only decelerate, and use that information to your advantage when you are out to win.

THE ATTAQUE POSITION

In the illustration you see me in what I can best describe as a position of *attaque*! My posture is active and alert. I'm ready to move quickly and forcefully in any direction. I can drive forward if I sense the need to. Or I can sit back, if I feel the need to make my back edges bite more. Again, I could step sideways if I felt that would be an advantage. In short, I'm ready to attack in any direction.

What is this position? Basically, it is standing on your skis so that your weight rests squarely and evenly on both feet, without pressing forward or backward. The hips are kept centered over both skis. And, very important is the bend at the waist which keeps the weight of the shoulders forward slightly—where it can easily be controlled. And, to help keep the shoulders forward—well, look at my hands and arms. It's an almost certain rule in ski racing that if you can't see your hands in front of you, you're heading for trouble.

I have called this a position, but you must understand that no good skier ever skis in *a* position. He is always moving, always adjusting, ever on the alert. Please, do not try to ski in a position that you see in the illustration. It is merely a guideline, and only a part of my style. But do try to ski with a slight bend at the waist—not as much as I have here—but enough to make it easy for you to attack.

DUAL RACING

For many people, watching a slalom or giant slalom race is rather dull. For one thing, these events offer little possibility for something dangerous to happen. For another, the competition is against the clock. Only one racer is on the course at any one time, and since the events are often won by mere hundredths of a second, it takes a very experienced eye indeed to appreciate the subtleties of the true champions.

In recent years, however, dual races—either slalom or giant slalom—have become increasingly popular, especially among the professionals. In these events, two competitors race against each other, man-to-man, through the gates of two almost identically set courses. Both competitors start at the same moment and the first to finish is the winner—of that heat. Then, to keep the competition fair, the racers swap courses—it is not possible to set the gates absolutely identical to one another because of uneven variations in the terrain. The racer who wins both heats, or who wins two out of three heats, is the winner.

Believe me, it is a much more exciting event to watch than the standard forms of Alpine competition because you see who wins and why. And it is very exciting to compete in, too; because you are always aware that the other racer is just ahead of you, or behind you, putting pressure on you either way.

DUCK AROUND THE POLE

Here, you see me coming fast at the slalom pole around which I must turn sharply. In the first figure note how my outside arm and shoulder are leading the way by twisting ever so slightly toward the turn. My weight is on the outside ski on the turn, helping it to carve in a track that will keep my skis close to the pole. I aim so close to that pole that I'd hit it with my chest or face if I hadn't trained myself to duck around just a split second before collision. This action is sometimes called reversed-shoulder because the shoulders appear to turn in the direction opposite to that of the skis. But be careful, the action must not make the skis turn more or faster, as a true reversed-shoulder motion would do. It is only a ducking around-and-down movement of the shoulder closest to the pole. Note that the other arm and shoulder are not allowed to move back much at all. In fact, the outside arm and hand even come up and forward as I duck. The movements are very much like those experienced when running and you duck or dodge around a tree or the corner of a building. Once you've mastered this ducking technique, it's guaranteed to knock seconds off your over-all time. It's another detail worth concentrating on, if you want to win.

THE SNEAKY STEP-UP

What you see me doing—stepping up for speed—is not something for every skier to try. It's basically a racer's maneuver designed to give a bit of extra speed. It does this in two ways: First, it gives you an extra foot or two of height before going into the turn; Second, it puts you in a better position to carve close to the next gate.

In the first figure, most of my weight rests on my lower ski, and I've begun to let my upper ski sneak uphill. In the second figure, I've planted my pole and actually transferred my weight to the uphill ski, which immediately becomes the outside ski of this new turn.

I could have kept my skis relatively close together throughout the turn, and then suddenly stepped up, as the small diagram illustrates. However, the "sneaky" approach seems to work more efficiently.

In the third figure, notice how my upper body has begun to move downhill, in the direction of the turn. Also notice how I have rolled my upper ski to change the edge on which it rests. That's the hardest part of this turn, and you'll have to practice hard and long to perfect the skill.

The remainder of the turn is accomplished like any other carving christie, and the skis are brought closer together to make it easy to get ready for . . . maybe another sneaky step up.

PLAN AHEAD—WAY AHEAD

It's surprising how long it took me to learn such a simple lesson as this—to win, you have to plan ahead. Now, I'm not referring to all the planning that must go on long before a race, or even the planning you must so thoroughly do just before you run down a course, such as memorizing the exact relationship of one slalom gate to another, although that is very important. I'm talking about the planning that must go on while you are actually racing down the course. And it's the same kind of planning that goes on even when the good skier skis for fun.

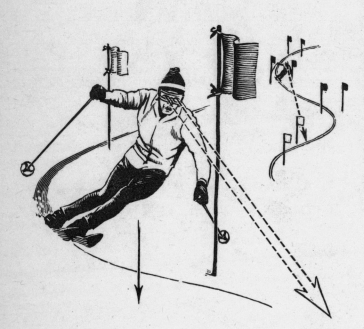

I'm referring to the importance of planning your course, and the only way to do this, whether going fast through a forest of slalom poles or a slope filled with moguls is to be ahead of yourself. How? By looking ahead to where you will soon be, by at least one turn, and maybe even two. The good skier or racer never worries about where he is, but concentrates on where he will be. You too must constantly look ahead, looking for the exact spot to start your turn, the exact rut to avoid or to make your skis follow. You must make your decisions before you get there, so that your body has time to react correctly when you do get there. Otherwise, you'll always be struggling to keep up with yourself. To become a really good skier, you must train yourself to ski with that kind of instant pre-planning. I did—after a good ten years of practice. Surely you can better that record.

TO WIN—HOLD YOUR TUCK

To win consistently in any sport, somewhere along the line you will have had to concentrate on every facet of what you do, so that bit by bit certain details become habitual. When racing downhill, for example, you must concentrate so hard on keeping your skis on the fastest line there is no time to think of technique. Therefore, you must practice your tuck position constantly—while skiing slowly, or fast, or even while standing in front of a mirror. You must learn to keep your back flat—in line with the skis—even when you rise up to give the legs a momentary rest, as you see me doing in the illustration. Note that my head is kept low also, and that the elbows are brought in close to the chest.

Train yourself to keep your arms in the position that you see mine in, and be very, very careful to keep the ski poles streamlined to your direction. I believe I've won many a downhill race simply because I was able to keep my tuck and the poles in proper position. I did everything possible to cut down on the slowing effects of wind resistance.

For a dramatic lesson about these effects, try this: Next time you are motoring along at downhill speeds of 60 or 70 mph, carefully hold an arm (and perhaps a ski pole) outside the car window. In fact, have the driver go only 40 mph first, accelerating gradually. You'll be amazed at the force of the wind—the same forces that you must overcome while skiing. So to win in downhill, concentrate on and master the details of holding a good, streamlined, tuck position.

A FUN TURN—MAMBO

Go about it in a sensible way, and skiing is fun right from the start. Amazingly, it continues becoming more pleasurable as you improve. That's particularly true once you crack the "parallel barrier." That's when without thinking about it you turn both skis at exactly the same instant. When that time comes along, you are ready to vastly expand your horizons for pleasure. Something about skiing parallel allows you to overcome almost every situation you'll encounter, perhaps because there are so many ways you can move your body to make your skis turn. And that, of course, means your body can mold itself to the changes in terrain.

One of these ways is with a turn called the mambo christie. It's great fun because the way the body is moved is so contrary to what is usually learned. Using the accompanying illustrations as a guide, follow me through the turn, step by step.

ONE: Traverse a smooth, packed slope. Pick up enough speed to make a christie—at least 10 mph. Twist your body downhill, toward the direction of the turn. But do not yet unweight or release the edges. In other words, do not let the twisting action affect the direction of the skis.

TWO: Now, the moment of truth—let the twisting action go right down through the hips to the feet and skis. At the same time make either an up or down unweighting movement and begin to lean or bank into the turn.

THREE: The instant the skis start to swivel around, start twisting the upper body in the *opposite* direction. This is called reversing the shoulders.

FOUR: Use this reversing action as the wind-up preparation for your next mambo christie.

It's weird, but fun. Try it.

FREESTYLE OR EXHIBITION SKIING

An amazing thing happened to ski competitions several years ago.

A whole new form of our sport has taken shape. It's called freestyle or exhibition skiing, and it was started by Doug Pfeiffer, a famous ski writer and good friend of mine.

What you see in the illustrations are skiers in each of the three phases of this kind of competition—aerial acrobatics, on-the-snow tricks, and just plain good fast skiing on very bumpy terrain. The uppermost illustration shows a skier doing the daring Javelin turn, with one ski crossed over the other. The middle figure shows an aerial acrobat doing a beautiful spread-eagle or split jump. The bottom skier is moving through a turn at more than 25 mph with only the heels of his skis dragging on the snow. This maneuver is called a wheelie.

Each contestant is given maximum freedom of expression in this new kind of ski competition, and does not have to compete against the clock, as in the traditional forms of ski racing. It's a do-your-own-thing kind of event and as a result it is just filled with suspense and excitement. It is great fun to watch. I know, because I have served as a judge for the U.S. National Freestyle Championships. Five people judge each contestant, and to alleviate the affects of possible bias by the judges, both the highest and lowest scores are tossed out and the three remaining scores are totalled.

I think you will like these events, and I also think that you should go back to ski school even if you are already a good skier and learn some of these new, exciting ways to get even more pleasure from your ski holidays.

YOU TOO CAN BE A "POWDER BUFF"

If you've done it, you know. If you haven't, you must take my word for it: Deep powder skiing can be one of life's most exciting experiences. You, too, can be a "Powder Buff!" You hear only the softest sound from your skis as they slip through the snow. The sensation of that snow as it brushes past your legs is soft, silky, even feathery. On hard snow, you may make a mistake—catch an edge as skiers say—but that will usually distract your ski only for a minute or two. Then you can pull it back into line. But in the deep powder, a mistake can actually cause you to catch your whole ski, and the pressure of the snow makes it hard to pull it back into line. As a result, you often end up—well, up-ended!

But don't let this problem scare you away from the powder snow. To handle it correctly, first learn to stand on your skis, but not the same way you do on packed snow. Learn to keep your weight distributed evenly on your feet. If your bindings are mounted too far forward or if the fronts of your skis are too stiff, it may be necessary to sit back slightly so that your weight presses back on your heels. At first, learn to schuss straight down a gentle powder slope. Keep weight slightly more on your heels. This is different from schussing on hard-pack where you must keep slightly more weight on the fronts of the skis. If there are none of those gentle powder slopes around, learn to traverse steep slopes of powder. Remember—keep your weight evenly distributed on both feet—that's different than traversing on the hard pack where you carry more weight on the lower ski. Also, don't be afraid to ski fast in the powder, for it is when you are moving at a fast clip and your skis are planing that the turns become easier and hence, more pleasurable. Do take care, however, when skiing in areas where hidden obstacles could be present. A buried fallen tree could spoil more than an afternoon on the slopes!

There are other differences between powder and packed snow skiing. In powder you must use more up and down movement to facilitate turning the skis. Also, it's almost a necessity that you keep your legs and feet tightly together in the powder. Since it takes a great deal of strength to turn your skis one at a time in the powder, it is almost indispensible that you learn to make parallel christies. For that I recommend taking lessons. Once you know how to make parallel christies you'll find you can easily adapt and adjust your technique for hard snow or powder. But if you can't make parallel christies you will never taste the real joys of deep powder skiing.

LEARN THE GELAENDESPRUNG; EASIER TO DO THAN PRONOUNCE

Strange the way language works, isn't it? I understand that in English you use a German word to describe what I'm doing here, while in French we use a Norwegian word. Americans say *"gelaendesprung"*—I hear some Americans even say *"gelandy"*—and we French say *"op-trakken."* Regardless of the words, what I'm going to tell you about is the terrain jump, so-called to distinguish it from the classic, prepared ski jump.

Nowadays, a terrain jump is usually done for the fun of flying through the air for five, 10, maybe even 100 feet. However, it wasn't always this way. In the early days of skiing, up to about 1935, skiers (for their own safety) had to jump over partially hidden fences, over roofs of Alpine hay huts, off small cliffs, and sometimes even across small streams or gaping crevasses in the glaciers. In those days, prepared courses were rare indeed. Now, it's only necessary to make a terrain jump when you're skiing fast and must avoid a big bump. A gelaendesprung is fun, however, because of the confidence you develop in knowing that you can jump if you have to, and because of the *joie de vivre* that comes from being airborne.

In the illustration, you see me jumping through space with my legs partially tucked up underneath me. This ski-tips-down position looks spectacular, and puts my skis parallel to the slope, ready for a smooth landing. I must point out that before my skis touch the ground, I extend my legs. They must be able to bend fully to absorb the shock of landing. Remember—the flatter the landing slope, the greater the shock will be.

To learn a gelaendesprung, look for a small bump—about a foot high—which is followed by a landing slope that's smooth for at least three ski lengths. It should not be pitched at anything less than 15 degrees. Climb up the slope a short distance and begin to ski down toward the take-off spot. On your first few attempts, don't try to spring off—merely let yourself sail through the air for a ski length or so. The first thing to develop is confidence and balance in the air. Do this by maintaining the same position you had at the moment of take-off. If the landing is quite steep, however, you will have to lean your body forward while airborne so that your skis won't shoot out from under you when you land.

As your confidence grows, try going faster. Next, learn to crouch down as you approach take-off point, then spring up quickly the instant your ski tips reach the edge of the bump. You'll have to practice this to learn the correct timing. As you practice, learn to judge the approximate distance you will fly through the air from any given bump and at different speeds. The confidence you'll gain from practicing gelaendesprungs will amaze you. Before long, you, too, will be able to perform a tip-drop leap like the one I demonstrate here.

4-Questions and Answers

Following is a compilation of questions most frequently asked of Olympic World Champion, Jean-Claude Killy. Like most great athletes, his answers to such purging are brief, thorough and authoritative. Slightly chauvinistic, Killy strongly defends French systems, products, etc., but at no time has he deprecated any other product nor put down any other skier for differences in style, theory or technique. He is a true champion in every sense of the word.

WEIGHT DISTRIBUTION

Q. Is it true that you ski with your weight distributed on both skis equally, rather than mostly on the downhill ski?

A. Yes, most of the time my weight is on both skis, but there are many exceptions. Sometimes my weight is on the uphill ski, as for example when I come out of a gate too low and must skate up. When I sit back, often my weight will be on the downhill ski.

The point is, I don't decide in advance where my weight is going to be. I adapt myself to the terrain. I weight the skis equally, or I weight the uphill or downhill ski, or I sit back or go forward—all as needed. Versatility is what makes the great skier.

ARE ARMS IMPORTANT?

Q. What part do the arms play in competition skiing?

A. The arms are quite important. On icy slopes, you frequently need to dig in with your poles. And in downhill, how you carry your arms is important to your speed. Wind tunnel experiments have shown you can lose seconds by holding the arms too far from the body. We sewed our bibs (racing numbers) to our jackets and wore tighter clothing after we saw the results of those tests.

But you can't always ski in an optimum aerodynamic position. The arms are needed for balance, and they must be ready for poling. That's why strengthening the arms must not be neglected in any conditioning program.

CHOICE OF SKI LENGTH

Q. In a film I saw of you skiing, I noticed you used two different ski lengths. What are the different conditions that determine your choice?

A. I use different lengths according to the different events, the different kinds of races, not for different kinds of snow conditions. For slalom, I always use 207 cm. For GS, I've used 212 or 215 cm. And for downhill, I've used everything from 219 to 230 cm., though I've found 220 cm. to be best for me. For recreational skiing, I generally use something around 210 cm. As you might guess, the general rule should be, the faster you ski, the longer the ski should be; the more turns you make, the shorter it should be—provided it is long enough to give you stability at the speed you want to go.

ARE WOOD SKIS COMPETITIVE?

Q. Would a racer today stand any chance of winning an event if he were using one of the topnotch wood skis that racers used a decade ago?

A. Provided he were racing against others of roughly the same ability, he would stand no chance of scoring a good time.

RELAXATION

Q. How do you relax before a race?

A. Relaxing before a race is simply a matter of knowing you have done everything you could to prepare properly for the race.

PHILOSOPHY OF A SKIER

Q. Andre Maurois wrote, "The body of an athlete and the soul of a wise man—this is what is needed to be happy." Is skiing a source of wisdom in itself—a world or the world in miniature—or is it an escape from the demands of life?

A. For me, skiing is a world in itself. It's close to nature—but there's nothing miniature about it. Everyone must find his own answer, but for me, I enjoy skiing for its own sake, not as an escape from anything.

WHY HAVEN'T U.S. SKIERS DONE WELL?

Q. Why do you think U.S. men skiers have not done so well in international competition?

A. Back in 1964, when Bill Kidd and Jim Heuga won their Olympic silver and bronze medals at Innsbruck, I thought the U.S. team really had it made. All the guys were going to college, and still they were in the top of the international class racing brackets. Well, now I'm not sure. It's a big handicap not to ski all of the time. Maybe it's better that the Americans do go to school, but I think that is why they are not able to beat the Europeans who ski 100 percent of the time.

FASTEST SPEED

Q. What's the fastest you ever skied?

A. I went to Cortina one summer to compete in the speed trials. But I had the wrong equipment, so I didn't do very well. The fastest I reached was 160 kilometers an hour (just under 100 mph).

EXTRA SPEED

Q. In a number of your races in the Killy Challenge, you seemed to be even with your opponent up to the last gate and then managed to get an extra burst of speed to beat him. How did you do that?

A. Though it may seem that a race is won between the last gate and the finish line, that is rarely the case. The momentum builds up for several gates beforehand. In the Killy Challenge, it is possible the camera angle created the illusion that I was winning with a sudden burst of speed.

Of course, there are things a racer can do to pick up fractions of seconds at the finish line. I always study where the electric eye is to see whether it will help to jet my skis out in front at the finish. I also check to see whether the finish line is parallel to the last gate. If not, I might shave a hundredth of a second off my time by coming out of that gate close to the pole that is nearest the finish line.

THE BIGGEST THREAT

Q. In the Killy Challenge, who posed the biggest threat?

A. Because of the handicap system, all were threats. But Pepi Stiegler was the one who came closest to beating me. First of all, he was familiar with racing over parallel courses. Secondly, he was in good shape. And finally, he is still a very strong, very dangerous skier.

MEMORIZE THE COURSE?

Q. Must a racer memorize a slalom course?

A. Though you don't have to memorize a whole course, it is necessary to memorize the traps and places where you have to change rhythm. Otherwise you may not know where you have to slow down, where it would be suicidal to go all out. But in practicing slalom, it's best not to memorize a course so that you can develop your instincts and reflexes.

BOOTS—RIGID OR NOT?

Q. On a downhill course, should your boots give some play to the ankles, or is it best to have complete rigidity?

A. Personally, I like my boots to be unyielding. But I know some very good racers who never fasten the top buckle when they run downhill so they'll have some play. It's whatever gives you the best control that counts.

RACING HEAD-TO-HEAD

Q. Do you prefer racing head-to-head, as the pros do, and as you did on the Killy Challenge, to racing the clock as the amateurs do?

A. I like them both. I like being alone on the course, going all out for the best time. But I also like the excitement of the man-to-man event. In any case, I think the future belongs to the parallel courses because it is so much more interesting for the TV viewer.

IS SKIER'S HEIGHT IMPORTANT?

Q. Do you have to be tall to be a good downhiller?

A. No. Karl Schranz, one of the world's greatest downhillers, is not tall. Neither is Henri Duvillard nor Leo Lacroix nor any number of other fine downhillers. Technique, not height, is what counts. Some people say that if you are heavier, you have an advantage in acceleration, but on the other hand, your skis might sink into the snow more. There are many theories on the subject, but I've never seen any proofs. All I know is that both small men and big men have won downhill races.

OBSESSION WITH SPEED

Q. When did you decide to be a ski racer?

A. There was no particular moment when I decided upon that direction. I received my first skis when I was five and have spent most of my life on them. My obsession with speed on skis prompted my parents to nickname me Toutoune, for I have always attacked the sport like a wild dog.

FIRST VICTORY

Q. Where and when was your first skiing victory?

A. There were many unofficial contests, between myself and the other children of Val d'Isere, but my first competition avec dossard was for a cup presented by Holland's Queen Juliana. The event was slalom. I was eight years old.

FORM IS NOT AS IMPORTANT AS SPEED

Q. You have been criticized for your lack of form and seeming awkwardness racing through the gates. Do you deprecate the final forms reached by ski instructors?

A. I have the ability to imitate anyone's ski form. If I choose to stray from picture perfect style for a moment in lieu of losing my spontaneity and speed, it is because I race to win. The clock is the final arbiter in any racing event, not the camera.

INJURIES

Q. Have you ever broken a leg?

A. In my early teens, when ski boots were too soft to offer my ankle protection, and bindings were still primitive, I competed for the Ilio Colli Cup at Cortina d'Ampezzo in Italy and suffered a minor fracture. My three months of recuperation only stoked the coals of competition which burned inside me. In less than half a year I was racing again. Ironically, I broke my leg again at the Ilio Colli in early 1962, which prevented me from competing for the World Championships at Chamonix that year.

FIRST INTERNATIONAL WIN

Q. When did you win your first international competition and in what event?

A. That was a slalom contest, the Grand Prix de Morzine, in 1961. It was a memorable occasion, culminating in a much more prized award: that of the rooster, official emblem of the French team.

MOST FORGETABLE PERFORMANCE

Q. Have you ever felt discouraged with any of your performances?

A. I would like to erase the memory of the 1964 Olympics at Innsbruck. Placing only fifth in the GS event, I was eliminated in the Slalom and Downhill contest. It may sound like sour grapes, but I honestly feel that inferior equipment and its maintenance were partly to blame. I was also racing against an amebic dysentery affliction which really sapped me.

MOST EXCITING RACE

Q. Does any one race stick in your mind as the most exciting?

A. That would have to be the second run at Kitzbuhel in 1965. Karl Schranz took the first race by 1.38 seconds, but he was 3 full seconds behind me in the second event. I also took the Combined Medal that year. This is to say nothing of my World Champion victory at Portillo, Chile in 1966, which of course, I shall never forget. The French team was awarded sixteen of twenty-four medals. It took a long time for someone to depose the formidable Austrians.

STAYING IN SHAPE

Q. What do you advise for staying in shape off season?
A. For most racing champions, there is no "off season." Somewhere in the world there is still snow, and that is where we go to train. Should this be impractical for you, try bicycling or just plain running. Don't avoid the hills while biking; there's always a downhill "reward," if you're patient. And, try running off the track, where various obstacles will train your reflexes along with your legs. Progressive weight lifting is also good for any athlete, for non-athletes, too, I might add. There is a popular misconception that exercises which involve weights are just for mesomorphic Mr. Universe types. A logical progressive system of weight lifting will not only improve your appearance beyond that of the common man, it will develop the muscles you need to ski more proficiently than him also.

THE RIGHT WAX

Q. How important is wax?
A. Champions are well tuned machines whose victorious performances are dependent upon every detail of preparation. Often, only hundredths of a second separate a World Champion from second place. The right wax can make the difference. For a recreational skier, too, the right wax can mean the difference between a smooth graceful descent and a choppy staccato run. Vary your wax with the temperature and with the condition of the snow, as described on the box in which it is packaged. My good friend and coach Michel Arpin conditions my skis with wax and proper sharpening before every race. I share my victories with him.

KILLY VS. ERIKSEN

Q. In a race between you and Stein Eriksen at the peak of his career, who would win?
A. It would not be ethical for me to pass judgement publicly upon so great a champion as Stein. The question came up between interviews several years ago, when Frank Covino and I were traveling with the International

Ski Show that tours your country each Fall. Frank assisted Stein in many of his "chalk-talk" lectures, was an instructor in Eriksen's ski school and is a close friend of the Norwegian champion. He had this to say: "In a modern race, Killy would take the cup. As a skiing stylist, whose perfection of form is inimitable, Stein is still King. The very characteristics of counterpoint that make Stein's form so beautiful to watch are diametrically opposed to the requirements of maximum speed and daring. The quality of skis and boots, to say nothing of the sophistication of ski racing technology, has advanced so rapidly in the past two decades that a comparison between the two champions is invalid. Giants of different eras should be appreciated within their chronological realms; one does not 'compare' Ingres to Picasso." While I am not certain that I appreciate Covino's selection of those particular artists for comparison, I do agree with the wisdom of his statement.

RECOMMENDS INSTRUCTION

Q. Were you ever enrolled in a ski school class?
A. While I have never had that experience, I highly recommend it for anyone who begins to ski at a later age. I started before school age, skied every day and had masters like Henri Oreiller around to guide me. You will progress faster and more safely if you take a steady diet of competent ski instruction.

SKIS AND BOOTS

Q. Which is more important, skis or boots?
A. The best tuned skis in existence must still be guided, first by your eyes, then your brain, then your thighs and knees and finally, by your boots. If your goal is to be "the best," let each of these items be "the best" you can acquire.

BEST BRAND

Q. Which brand is best?
A. As a Frenchman, I am naturally in favor of French products, although we did not have a strong contender for the best ski until 1966, after I proved to my country's ski manufacturers that the French could win with the right skis; I raced on Austrian skis at the Megeve downhill and won. Since the development of fibreglass technology and the improvement of French equipment which helped me win the World Championship downhill, many brands have changed their ski construction for your advantage. Unfortunately the price of the equipment is usually commensurate with its performance, whether you are considering boots or skis. As far as boots are concerned, function and form run a close race for major concern. A good performing boot is of little use to you if it does not fit properly. I suppose your American expression "try, before you buy" is the most sensible answer I can give to your question.

SKIS TOGETHER OR APART?

Q. My ski instructor keeps his skis tightly together, yet almost every photo I've seen of you shows your skis apart. Which is right?

A. What is "right" for me might not be right for your ski instructor. He is paid to look elegant, poised and graceful. I am paid to win races. At the speeds with which I travel independent leg action is absolutely essential. I find a stance with the skis apart most effective for me, although I keep them close together in deep powder.

UNWEIGHTING

Q. Which is better, to unweight with a down motion or with an up motion?

A. Unweighting is an important element of every turn, but whether you choose up or down is arbitrary and entirely dependent upon the particular situation. For example, a bump or rise in the surface will automatically cause what appears to be a moment of down unweighting, if your knees are flexible. What actually happens is that your knees are forced upward towards your chest; your derriere appears to drop. We call this movement avalement, referring to the "swallow" of the mogul by the knees. Another method of turning over the bumps is to first check the edges sharply and then bounce the tails upward to allow the ski tips to carve the turn; this is a form of unweighting with an up motion, more popular in the fifties. One thing remains constant: the skis are turned when they are in an unweighted state. Up or down is your choice.

GLISSEMENT

Q. Georges Joubert has written that "the art of skiing resides in the sliding of the skis–what in France we call glissement." Do you agree?

A. Sliding the skis requires little skill, as gravity is the prime mover. To be able to carve a turn with the skis on their edges is the "art" of skiing.

ANGULATION

Q. Is angulation necessary?

A. Fail to angulate on an icy steep slope and you'll soon know the answer. In deep "bottomless" powder you may bank your turns because the pull of gravity downhill is not as great, but as that pull increases with faster packed terrain, you had better drop your downhill shoulder. A good general rule is to keep your shoulders about the same slant as the hill, especially if you ski with your skis close together.

FACE DIRECTION OF TRAVEL

Q. Should I face in the direction my skis are pointed, at all times?

A. A good skier looks toward the direction in which he is traveling, downhill and well ahead of his next turn. Your skis are often not pointed in that direction.

SKIING NEW POWDER

Q. Should I sit back when skiing through new powder snow?

A. If the depth of the new snow is a foot or under, your technique need not be modified, but if the powder is waist deep or more, it is important to plane the tips of your skis upward or they will dive and bury you. Above all, keep your body weight equally distributed and turn both skis as a single unit in deep powder.

WEIGHT ON DOWNHILL SKI

Q. Should my weight always be on my downhill ski?

A. To get a higher faster line into a gate I frequently step uphill weighting my uphill ski for a moment. There are other times when it may be practical to stray from tradition, as in powder snow, when you had better keep your weight equal on both skis.

AVALEMENT

Q. Is avalement the best method of skiing a mogul run?

A. If your thighs are strong and your knees are flexible. It also takes an exceptionally strong stomach. Should your knees and footwork be fast, try what you Americans call "running the river," checking your speed against the uphill side of the mogul and sliding through the groove between it and the next bump, but be sure to keep your hips and shoulders perpendicular to the fall line at all times. Variation of method will enhance your style and make your skiing more enjoyable. There is nothing more insipid than a skier making the same kind of turn from the top of the trail to the bottom.

THE MOST COMMON ERROR

Q. What is the most common error you have detected among tyro racers?

A. Entering a gate too low. This forces the racer to check his speed with a traverse that practically has him starting the next turn with no momentum at all. Watch how often a pro scissors his ski tips for a moment, stepping uphill to get a faster line, a higher line to enter the next gate at maximum velocity.

THE REVERSE SHOULDER

Q. Whatever happened to "reverse shoulder"?

A. Reverse shoulder is alive and well and evident in every racing turn that brings the skier close to the inside gate. If the inside shoulder does not lead, it will smash into the pole and cost you some time. Extreme exaggeration of the position led to the mannerist Austrian and Stein Eriksen variation for recreational skiing, very popular in the fifties and early sixties. Since then, ski schools all over the world have adopted a less extreme counterpoint of the upper body, with the shoulders reversed only as much as the skis. To be more explicit, as the uphill or inside ski leads the downhill or outside ski by a few inches, so also does the inside boot, knee, hip and shoulder follow the same length of lead, for recreational skiing today.

ANTICIPATION

Q. What is meant by "anticipation"?

A. It is basically an initiation of the turn by a movement of the upper body toward the fall line, coupled with either an up or down motion to release bodyweight from the skis. Since I believe in always facing the fall line I am in constant anticipation each time I plant my pole and attack my turn.

Anticipation is perhaps the foremost characteristic of modern skiing.

TURNING ON ICE

Q. Whenever I turn on ice or boilerplate my skis slide wide apart and I skid for yards before catching my new traverse. What am I doing wrong?

A. You probably are throwing your hip to the outside of the turn, *mon ami*. Touch your downhill pole as you anticipate your new direction but lead the turn with your inside hip once you reach the fall line and begin to angulate strongly with your bodyweight mostly on the center of your downhill ski. Also, you should reduce your down-up motion when preparing for a turn on the ice; rely more upon your knees and your feet to turn the skis.

SKIING ON "CRUD"

Q. What about skiing "crud"? We get a lot of garbage conditions in the east; you know: ice cubes, breakable crust . . .

A. Stay on both feet and jump your turns around. This may not be a graceful maneuver, but it is the safest way to handle such *conditions mal*.

TO START RACING

Q. How can I begin racing?

A. Most ski schools terminate their ski week programs with a race between students. This is a great way to improve your skiing with qualified instruction and get the feel of competition and perhaps victory at the end of your effort. Beyond this, look into organizations such as the Canadian Ski Instructors Alliance, if you live in Canada, or the various Ski Instructors Associations of the United States, like the United States Eastern Amateur Ski Association, the Central U.S. Ski Instructors Association, the Rocky Mountain Ski Instructors Association or the Far West Ski Instructors Association. Your local ski school director can guide you.

EFFORTLESS MOGUL SKIING

Q. What is the most effortless way to ski over a mogul?

A. Probably using the turn called *le serpent* by Georges Joubert. Assume a balanced upright position between the moguls. When your ski tips reach the top of the bump, plant your inside pole on the downhill side of the mogul facing your upper body to the fall line. Then, relax allowing your upper body to tip forward between your skis and your planted pole. Bend your knees to absorb the bump and your skis will slide effortlessly into the turn. This turn is very effective in rutted slalom runs also, in case you should get a late starting number.

SLIDING ON THE EDGES

Q. I have heard it said that you are a master of glissement. *Can you translate?*

A. *Glissement* refers to the sliding of the skis, but not necessarily on their bottoms. A good racer has mastered *glissement* on the edges of his skis, remaining in continuous contact with the snow. Get into the air and you will lose vital seconds.

STIFFNESS ON TURNS

Q. What can I do to correct a stiffness I experience just before every turn? I am just beginning to parallel.

A. Try to loosen up by bouncing your ski tails off the snow as you traverse. Add an anticipatory movement of your upper body to the last bounce and your skis will automatically turn.

TOO OLD TO START?

Q. Am I too old to ski? (This question is frequently asked by men and women from teens to over-forties. Ed.)

A. If you can see, if you can think, and if you can run, you are capable of learning how to ski; add to those requirements the important prerequisite of desire, and you will learn very quickly.

PROPER CAMBER

Q. How much camber should my skis have?

A. Skis with too much camber will be difficult to turn in most good snow conditions. Place your skis together, bottom to bottom, and measure the space between. An inch to one and a half inches is sufficient.

OLD SKIS

Q. My skis get worse every year. They don't seem to slide into the turns. They want to go straight all the time. Should I put them out to pasture?

A. All that may be necessary is a good flat filing. The bottoms of skis will sometimes cave-in, allowing the edges to ride lower. I think you Americans call this "railing." A railed ski will track straight unless it is powered by a great effort. Flat-file the bottoms and keep them that way.

GOGGLES ARE IMPORTANT

Q. How important are goggles?

A. As important as your eyes, they can even affect your race. A dark lens will protect your eyes from sunburn on a very bright day, while yellow lenses will cheer up a foggy day by bathing it with simulated sunshine. Yellow goggles will also darken the mogul shadows. Goggles also have a tunneled vision effect that will help keep your eyes on the course and away from the *jeune filles* on the sidelines.

FRENCH DOMINANCE

Q. How do you account for the sudden emergence of France as a major skiing power?

A. It would have happened before, had we had better equipment and more informative ski racing technology. Now that we have, France will continue to be a *formidable* contender.

A FINAL WORD

Q. Do you ever get sick of skiing?
A. *Alors!* Do you ever get sick of breathing?